FIRST PARAGRAPHS

Inspired Openings for
Writers and Readers

DONALD NEWLOVE

An Owl Book
Henry Holt and Company   New York

TO MY FELLOWSHIP OF WRITERS EVERYWHERE, SUNG AND UNSUNG, PUBLISHED AND UNPUBLISHED, PAID AND UNPAID

And to those who encourage us over the years,
among them my friends

Keith and Douglas Gunthardt   Alex and Mary Ionescu
Bob and Marge Vickrey   George and Muriel Castanis
Lou and Joan Ormont

———

Henry Holt and Company, Inc.
Publishers since 1866
115 West 18th Street
New York, New York 10011

Henry Holt® is a registered trademark
of Henry Holt and Company, Inc.

Published in Canada by Fitzhenry & Whiteside Ltd.,
91 Granton Drive, Richmond Hill, Ontario L4B 2N5.

Library of Congress Cataloging-in-Publication Data
Newlove, Donald.
First paragraphs : inspired openings for writers and readers /
Donald Newlove. — 1st Owl book ed.
      p.   cm.
Originally published: New York : St. Martin's Press, 1992.
"An Owl book."
1. Openings (Rhetoric)   2. Authorship.   I. Title.
PN3365.N48   1993
808'.02—dc20   93–21734
                                                      CIP

ISBN 0-8050-2597-9

First published in hardcover by St. Martin's Press in 1992.
First Owl Book Edition—1993

Designed by Glen M. Edelstein
Printed in the United States of America
All first editions are printed on acid-free paper. ∞
          1   3   5   7   9   10   8   6   4   2

> *Dear one, the world*
> *is waiting for the sunrise,*
> *Ev'ry rose*
> *is heavy with dew . . .*
> —Gene Lockhart

First paragraphs are written on Olympus. Whitehot shoes from the forge, they glow and ring on the anvil as a god batters them into shape. But even Vulcan's shop has its perils. Great writing is dangerous. It sings on the eyeball and wants to change our lives.

If you're a writer and burning to strike a great first paragraph—or just a reader with a crush on Homeric openings—perhaps this book will change your life. And mine! At least it should sharpen our ear about first chords in storytelling. I say "our" because I write for myself as well as you. I mean to test myself as well as the reader in these pages. So, if I say "we," I mean myself and the reader-perhaps-writer, or "we writers," the two of us. We write this book together, and may get burned.

I say craft is not enough. The writer has to be clear, has to get one breath beating in the ribs of writer and reader, and he must mean what he's saying. Craft may work strongly with one or two of these laws for great writing. But only all three together can bring about the to-and-fro of feelings between writer and reader that infects them both with a happy contagion called art.

Just as all great music at heart comes from dance, so the living sentence comes from breath. We write to a rhythm of breathing. A line must breathe. On bad days we choke our line with headstuff and try to slap life into stillborn wordage. On bad days we chop thoughts into lengths like so much hemp or clothesline. On good days these cords magically begin to breathe. Our lines slither and strike upward and infect. We are dangerous.

This is a book about first paragraphs, about the first welling of life that gives breath to a piece of writing. Suddenly a great sentence steals at us like a woman dancing the tango. Even if it's only one beat, one word. There's an orchid in her hair, hunger in her eye, and her heel comes down on the first fingersnap. *YOU—are mine!—YOU are MINE right NOW-W!* But allure is not all. It's breath that sets the beat. Without that she's just acting, showing us her teeth. Her hips don't light up our deepest fears.

This book means to be an energizer, a battery charge that boosts us straight from sleep to the word processor. A block of sheer uplift: we lay our hand on it and feel so good we want to die. Here comes a fresh charge of fast starts. Here come the virtuosos, their bare hands on the current, and their first paragraphs grabbing our shirts: *Listen to me.*

This is a handbook of the soul, not a chapbook on technique. It speaks to you from the gut upward, not just to your typing fingers. It's an essay in energy, the power that comes from a clear mind with a high purpose set on moving the reader. Somewhere herein a prickle should rush up your back and turn you whitehot to write.

This is the first paragraph of what I call the world's greatest short story:

The Assyrian King, Esarhaddon, had conquered the kingdom of King Lailie, had destroyed and burnt the towns, taken all the inhabitants captive to his own country, slaughtered the warriors, beheaded some chieftains and impaled or flayed others, and had confined King Lailie himself in a cage.

As he lay on his bed one night, King Esarhaddon was thinking how he should execute Lailie, when suddenly he heard a rustling near his bed and opening his eyes saw an old man with a long grey beard and mild eyes.

—"Esarhaddon, King of Assyria" (1903), Leo Tolstoy

This starts BIG, sweeps us through burning towns, shows us captives being marched to another country, prisoner warriors being slaughtered, chiefs beheaded or dropped onto stakes or having their skins whipped from their flesh, and then brings us down to the captured king in a cage.

All in one sentence!—a "synoptic" sentence. It's a synopsis of all that's happened before the first paragraph, and—as does Homer in *The Iliad*—it plunges us into the middle of some huge, wheeling and seemingly tragic action. But Tolstoy uses the epic voice only to draw us into his favorite subject: The inner life of an unawakened man. If Tolstoy is known for anything, it should be for his skill at turning his hero (and the unwary reader) inside out and sending him forth with his whole moral being reversed like a glove. He makes stunning art out of his surprise reversals, since he focuses on icy or petty or emptyheaded or socially chained men who have no head for change and are unlikely *ever* to change—and then he changes them, and changes us.

Unlike Emile Zola, whose *L'Assommoir* (1876) shows us a working-class mother degraded by alcohol, who is a failure at whoring and who at last dies under a staircase where no one notices her body for two days, Tolstoy in *Resurrection* (1899) finds a hardworking whore's downfall less gripping than her moral recovery. In fact, though he admired Zola, he thought

Zola's backhanded swat at moral reform in *L'Assommoir* an avoidance of a novelist's greater imaginative duty. To show the pit a woman has fallen into and then say "There's no help for her" is as sentimental as weeping over her and reading tracts aloud. The novelist's duty, to Tolstoy, is to show the way out of the pit. Just to show degraded beings is feeble or unfinished storytelling.

Aside from epic sweep, Tolstoy shares two qualities with Homer, not only in "Esarhaddon" but everywhere in his work. He looks down on his story from above, telling it with absolute mastery of its events. And he has infinite pity for his characters, including horses, bears, wolves and dogs. No character in Tolstoy or Homer is to be laughed at, denounced or degraded, or to be experienced by the reader with less than pity. All are in the grip of their author's overriding compassion.

"Esarhaddon" begins with a bloodbath—and gets bloodier! This blood underscores Tolstoy's purpose. He seems to say, "I show you man at his most depraved—in a king who enjoys slaughter and cutting off hands and ears and noses, and who lies on his bed toying with the bloodiest, most painful ways to execute his enemy king. A man utterly beyond moral change, for whom horror is sunlight." Tolstoy relishes the worst possible case and blackest human being for subject matter. He knows that such brittle, unyielding men are sitting ducks for change. The right tap will crack them.

"Esarhaddon" is the only out-of-print piece I talk about in *First Paragraphs* (aside from a novel of my own). So I'll tell you what happens in its seven pages. The mild-eyed man with the long grey beard tells Esarhaddon he cannot take Lailie's life since Lailie *is* Esarhaddon. What's more, the fourteen thousand warriors he has tormented, tortured and slaughtered aren't dead. They too are him, and life cannot be destroyed. Esarhaddon scoffs, but the old man says dip down your head and begins pouring a pitcher of water onto Esarhaddon's head. Suddenly, and with no surprise, Esarhaddon finds himself lying abed with Lailie's wife and being spoken to tenderly as Lailie.

His princes come and tell him about wicked King Esarhaddon, who has insulted him. Lailie (Esarhaddon) sends ambassadors to Esarhaddon, then rides out to hunt, kills two wild asses, a lioness, and captures her cubs. He feasts. His ambassadors return with their noses and ears lopped off by Esarhaddon. Lailie leads his troops against Esarhaddon but "the warriors of Lailie were but as hundreds, while those of Esarhaddon were as thousands, and Lailie feels himself wounded and taken prisoner." Ten days later he reaches Nineveh and is caged. He suffers shame and rage as his family and friends are led out to death: "He heard the groans of those who were executed; some had their hands and feet cut off, others were flayed alive . . . He saw the wife he loved, bound, and . . . taken as a slave to Esarhaddon." At last, groaning with despair, he is taken out to a sharp stake dripping with blood "from which the corpse of one of his friends had just been torn" and, stripped naked, his once strong, handsome body now startlingly lean, he is lifted up and about to be dropped on the stake. "This is death, destruction!" he thinks. "But this cannot be. Surely I am asleep. It is a dream." And rousing himself, he does indeed awake, only to find himself neither Esarhaddon nor Lailie but some astonishing kind of animal grazing in a valley "and brushing away flies with his long tail." Then a longlegged colt pokes "its smooth little muzzle" under his stomach and begins suckling. "Esarhaddon understood that he was a she-ass, the colt's mother, and this neither surprised nor grieved him, but rather gave him pleasure. He experienced a glad feeling of simultaneous life in himself and in his offspring." But suddenly something whistles toward him and sinks its sharp point into his skin and flesh. He tears the udder from the colt's teeth and gallops off to the herd. "The colt kept up with him, galloping by his side. They had already nearly reached the herd, which had started off, when another arrow in full flight struck the colt's neck. It pierced the skin and quivered in its flesh. The colt sobbed piteously and fell upon its knees. Esarhaddon could not abandon it, and remained standing over it. The colt rose, tottered on its long, thin legs, and again fell. A fearful two-legged being—a man—ran up and cut its throat." In horror Esarhaddon rouses himself again and the old man is just pouring over his head the last drops of the pitcher. He's terrified.

"Do you now understand," the old man asks, "that Lailie is you, and the warriors you put to death were you also? And not the warriors only, but the animals which you slew when hunting and ate at your feasts, were also you. You thought life dwelt in you alone, but I have drawn aside the veil. . . . Life is one in them all, and yours but a portion of this same common life. . . . To destroy the life that dwells in others is beyond your power. The life of those you have slain has vanished from your eyes, but is not destroyed. . . . Life knows neither time nor space. The life of a moment and the life of a thousand years, your life and the life of all the visible and invisible beings in the world, are equal . . . for life is the one thing that exists. All else, but seems to us to be." Esarhaddon stops the executions, gives his kingdom over to his son Assur-bani-pal, and becomes a wandering preacher, telling people "that all life is one, and that when men wish to harm others, they really do evil to themselves."

I like a story that doesn't fudge its message—and in which Tolstoy never flinches at what might be called fatheaded philosophy. Tolstoy's story comes out of his cells. It blooms from the daylight in which his body and mind live. It's not grist for a treatise. What lifts this tale up to heaven is its dumbfounding vividness, the details that like a colt nuzzle you all over, or like a human hand pinch you awake. You stand bare-ankled in streaming reality as it surges toward a falls just ahead. Although the story's argument would seem to be in the old man's speech at the end, its real argument takes place step by step in the glare of Tolstoy's imagination. Today we would probably lop off the old man's speech and let the story stand by itself on two bleeding ankle bones.

This is the last time we go so far afield of the first paragraph.

I did so to set the tone for the rest of the book. A great first paragraph is written clearly, it infects us with life, and it means what it says. By choosing Tolstoy first, who *always* means what he says, I show I mean what I say. What's more, Tolstoy's point is not that distant from today's idea that all life is one experiencing plasm whose existence reaches from prehistory into the unknown future, not bound by time in the human sense, and whose experience is deathless, no matter which cells fade away.

In *The Adventures of Huckleberry Finn*'s first paragraph, Mark Twain might seem to be only joshing. He was never more serious. Well, he was more serious, but unsuccessfully so, in *Joan of Arc* (1896), his longest novel, which he wrote late in life to show he could be serious. He's serious, but the characters rarely come to life, and their medieval talk never does. It remained Twain's favorite among his works, although—a devout cynic, and anti-Catholic—he writes about a Catholic saint. Indeed, when Joan burns at the stake, Twain burns with her—he couldn't write for days afterward. That's serious. But it's not enough.

> You don't know about me, without you have read a book by the name of "The Adventures of Tom Sawyer," but that ain't no matter. That book was made by Mr. Mark Twain, and he told the truth, mainly. There was things which he stretched, but mainly he told the truth. That is nothing. I never seen anybody but lied, one time or another, without it was aunt Polly, or the widow, and maybe Mary. Aunt Polly—Tom's aunt Polly, she is—and Mary, and the widow Douglas, is all told about in that book—which is mostly a true book; with some stretchers, as I said before.
> —*The Adventures of Huckleberry Finn* (1885), Mark Twain

Twain hooks us with humor because he knows he has some barbaric things to tell us later, and we might not hang around for those horrors if we knew they were coming. He revised *Huck Finn* heavily to make clear its theme of man's inhumanity to man and did it so strongly that when the book first appeared many librarians refused to stock it. At its most cutting, the satire in *Huckleberry Finn* equals in grisliness that of Jonathan Swift in *Gulliver's Travels*. Huck's travels are Twain's dark horselaugh at mankind.

The humor, though, holds the novel's largest theme, that all men lie or distort the truth, and some do so at a horrific cost to others. His first paragraph states clearly the theme of truthtelling: Huck's voice is infectious and lifelike, has a hard edge of wisdom to it, and Twain and Huck mean what they tell us.

Without fussing with dates, Twain sets his story sometime in the decade 1835–45. Huck's sadistic, drunken, nigger-hating, white-trash Pap, in a fit of alcoholic delirium, tries to kill him. Huck, who is a shrewd fourteen-year-old, flees home and teams up with Nigger Jim, who has fled being sold downriver and parted from his family. Their raft trip down the big Muddy, along with Melville's "The Three-Day Chase" that ends *Moby Dick*, are the highwatermarks of American storytelling. At one point Huck, up in a tree, watches the feud between the Grangerfords and the Shephersons end in murders and feels "so sick I almost fell out of the tree. I ain't agoing to tell *all* that happened—it would make me sick again if I was to do that. I wished I hadn't ever come ashore that night, to see such things. I ain't ever going to get shut of them—lots of times I dream about them."

Though Jim's flight to freedom engages us, an even richer theme is Huck's flight from the lies, hypocrisy and ugliness of civilization. Jim and Huck's idyll on the Mississippi is sullied by two con men who join them and set about bilking riverfolk. At the heart of Huck's sense of Paradise on the river is Twain's own escape from civilization's bindings in Hartford, Connecticut, where he'd settled down to married life. In writing his tale, Twain burst from spirit-stifling New England and found heroic energy in Huck's shrewd ruses as a con man and many roles as an actor. The first paragraph looks forward to Twain's own thoughts on the slave question as a Southerner whose heart fought against his Missouri upbringing. His split with himself heals fully in Huck's wrestling with his conscience and agonies about helping Jim escape. Twain himself says nothing, lets Huck say everything: "All right, then, I'll *go* to hell."

Twain's triumph is that his ravishing starry nights, river echoes, and fogs are matched in imaginative power by Huck's agonies over Jim and the raspings on his soul made by folks he meets along the river. Twain strikes this moral note in the first paragraph and Huck sets all down *without* stretchers. Huck does the truth-telling. He could hardly do less, since his name—a blending of wild berries and fish fins—tells us he is the outcast, humorless, anti-Christian, goat-eyed great god Pan who sees all truth like a runaway peering through the rushes. With this creation, as Huck wavers between the honey of life on his raft and the smell of burning pitch pine ashore, Twain is in paradise. A good place to kick off a first paragraph.

This is justly among the most beloved first paragraphs since World War II:

> If you really want to hear about it, the first thing you'll probably want to know is where I was born, and what my lousy childhood was like, and how my parents were occupied and all before they had me, and all that David Copperfield kind of crap, but I don't feel like going into it, if you want to know the truth. In the first place, that stuff bores me, and in the second place, my parents would have about two hemorrhages apiece if I told anything pretty personal about them. They're quite touchy about anything like that, especially my father. They're *nice* and all—I'm not saying that—but they're also touchy as hell. Besides, I'm not going to tell you my whole goddam autobiography or anything. I'll just tell you about this madman stuff that

happened to me around last Christmas just before I got pretty run-down and had to come out here and take it easy. I mean that's all I told D.B. about, and he's my *brother* and all. He's in Hollywood. That isn't too far from this crumby place, and he comes over and visits me practically every week end. He's going to drive me home when I go home next month maybe. He just got a Jaguar. One of those little English jobs that can do around two hundred miles an hour. It cost him damn near four thousand bucks. He's got a lot of dough, now. He didn't *use* to. He used to be just a regular writer, when he was home. He wrote this terrific book of short stories, *The Secret Goldfish*, in case you never heard of him. The best one in it was "The Secret Goldfish." It was about this little kid that wouldn't let anybody look at his goldfish because he'd bought it with his own money. It killed me. Now he's out in Hollywood, D.B., being a prostitute. If there's one thing I hate, it's the movies. Don't even mention them to me.

> —*The Catcher in the Rye* (1951), J. D. Salinger

The mention of *David Copperfield* at first veils from us that this paragraph could never have been written had there been no Huck Finn. Holden Caulfield, two years older than Huck, is so knotted up about telling the truth in a world full of phonies that his anguish lands him in a mental clinic. Huck Finn has sold out to civilization.

Deeply depressed, Holden has a more complex inner life than Huck. Where Huck's heart overcomes his conscience in helping Jim escape, and strengthens him, Holden struggles with a larger, less focused problem, his ongoing discovery that *everyone*—except his ten-year-old sister Phoebe—lies and cheats. Even his brother D.B., a wonderful writer, has become a Hollywood "prostitute," a screenwriter so rotten that Holden wants to puke when he even thinks of movies. This vomitous tide of hypocrites—call it a spiritual acne flooding and disfiguring his soul—so nauseates him that he flunks all his courses but English and gets expelled from Pencey Prep. He sells his typewriter, has a big wad of cash from his dotty grandmother who sends him birthday checks four times a year, and finds himself wandering about Manhattan for Christmas weekend, going nearly mad. Even so, where Huck's experience of mankind is black with death and doubledealing, Holden's is anguished and dreary while showing mankind as vile, worthless, and to be scorned.

Late in the novel Holden discloses a secret to Phoebe that lifts us back magnetically to the first paragraph. He tells her how attracted he is to Robert Burns's poem "If a body meet a body comin' through the rye":

> I thought it was "If a body catch a body" . . . Anyway, I keep picturing all these little kids playing some game in this big field of rye and all. Thousands of little kids, and nobody's around—nobody big, I mean—except me. And I'm standing on the edge of some crazy cliff. What I have to do, I have to catch everybody if they start to go over the cliff—I mean if they're running and they don't look where they're going I have to come from somewhere and *catch* them. That's all I'd do all day. I'd just be the catcher in the rye and all. I know it's crazy, but that's the only thing I'd like to be. I know it's crazy.

Even in such an idyll, saving the kids before they fall off the world into crap and become phonies, Holden is as alone as in daily life. He can't befriend or love a phony, only the innocent and pure of heart. He knows it's crazy, since everyone grows up and becomes impure. His spiritual agony lanced by his "goddam" perfectionism, he swears endlessly against his pain, and then, even he becomes a phony, "traveling incognito," passing himself off as twenty-two-year-old Jim Steele to a childlike prostitute in his hotel room.

The theme of saving the innocent comes to a head at Phoebe's school, when Holden wipes a "Fuck you" off the wall

("I wanted to kill whoever'd written it"), then finds a second "Fuck you" scratched in with a knife: "It wouldn't come off. It's hopeless, anyway. If you had a million years to do it in, you couldn't rub out even *half* the 'Fuck you' signs in the world. It's impossible." And here we find the paradise underpinning Salinger's first paragraph, since all of this has already happened to Holden before he starts the book. His first words to us are his badmouthing of a so-called children's classic, *David Copperfield*, while really he's clutching at his "lousy childhood" and rippling with birth agonies of adolescence. For Salinger it's heaven to have a character tell us clearly about his pain, to infect us with it, and to mean every word he confesses.

A variation on Huck and Holden:

IT'S SIX A.M.
DO YOU KNOW
WHERE YOU ARE?

You are not the kind of guy who would be at a place like this at this time of the morning. But here you are, and you cannot say that the terrain is entirely unfamiliar, although the details are fuzzy. You are at a nightclub talking to a girl with a shaved head. The club is either Heartbreak or the Lizard Lounge. All might come clear if you could just slip into the bathroom and do a little more Bolivian Marching Powder. Then again, it might not. A small voice inside you insists that this epidemic lack of clarity is a result of too much of that already. The night has already turned on that imperceptible pivot where two A.M. changes to six A.M. You know this moment has come and gone, but you are not yet willing to concede that you have crossed the line beyond which all is gratuitous damage and the palsy of unraveled nerve endings. Somewhere back there you could have cut your losses, but you rode past that moment on a comet trail of white powder and now you are trying to hang on to the rush. Your brain at this moment is composed of brigades of tiny Bolivian soldiers. They are tired and muddy from their

long march through the night. There are holes in their boots and they are hungry. They need to be fed. They need the Bolivian Marching Powder.
            —*Bright Lights, Big City* (1984), Jay McInerney

This lyric paragraph celebrates cocaine and, while Bolivian Marching Powder is a moving force in the novel, addiction is pretty much a subtheme. The main theme is the hero's self-dismemberment by surrender to false values. Addiction, meanwhile, is seen only in its early stages. The hero has lost his wife and loses his job, but he's not yet into habit-supporting ruses such as dealing and petty thievery, or into the hospitalizations, clinical depression, and bottoming out of character lying ahead for him. Even wifeless and jobless, he's still got plenty to spend, but the coke and booze soon will be gnawing at his reserves.

The paragraph glitters with the hero's seesawings between guilt and the rush of a hit. The first fuzzy notes come together with the reader set face to face with a girl with a shaved head in a nightclub. We hear the ornamental jangle of *The Great Gatsby*'s opening lines in this novel's opening "gratuitous damage and the palsy of unraveled nerve endings" (*Gatsby*: ". . . the abortive sorrows and short-winded elations of men"), and later, in the novel's closing lines, as the hero sits looking at the Hudson River in the dawn and awaits some kind of wisdom to cleave through his habit (*Bright Lights*: "You think of the wooden shoes of the first Dutch settlers on these same stones;" *Gatsby*: "I became aware of the old island here that flowered once for Dutch sailors' eyes—a fresh, green breast of the new world"). These are homages, and McInerney's unwavering brilliance in *Bright Lights, Big City* shows a faultless grip on style throughout. The hero ("You") is a fact-checker for a magazine like *The New Yorker* and the microscopic study of facts at which he works daily gives his present memoir authenticity: the reader is ever aware that the prose he's reading will have no gaffes of style or butchered grammar. In fact, we are treated to a first-novelist's *tour de force* of style, the kind of "look at my wares, my silks, my gold" that becomes an unrepeatably exuberant act that delighted readers will look forward to for the rest of McInerney's writing life and which, of course, he will never repeat—and shouldn't be expected to. One *Gatsby* is enough, one *Bright Lights*.

The nameless "You" is twenty-four (McInerney was twenty-three when his novel was published) and could be Holden Caulfield eight years later, as well. "You's" wife deserts him and his longings for her are the empty fallout after the death of a hit of coke. She *is* coke: Brainlessly ravishing, and he will never get that fine flush back that she granted him once. In his frazzled emptiness, "You" searches for something to fill him with hope, but all he has are his routine hangovers, failures at work, worthless notes toward a short story, and bizarre fixation on this week's continuing sob story in *The New York Post* about Coma Baby, a baby waiting to be born to a woman in a fatal coma. In the novel "You's" mother dies of cancer, in great pain, while resisting morphine. "You" respects his mother, and perhaps he too can resist cocaine and alcohol. He is, of course, Coma Baby, waiting to be reborn. So, rather than a novel largely about addiction, this is a story leading up to the rebirth which allows "You" to write the very book you now read. Where did McInerney begin when he wrote his first paragraph? From a sense of strength and power, but a different strength and power than the feelings of omnipotence that cocaine might provide. He began with a leap to he knew not where—"You are not the kind of guy who would be at a place like this at this time of the morning"—and found himself like an Olympic gymnast scoring a perfect ten in his first paragraph. Nice place to be.

Here's Huck Finn still again, the American Pan-spirit hurled into ink, bursting from the chains of a German upbringing in Brooklyn and, from the novelist's adolescence into his mid-thirties, attempting to screw every woman in sight:

Once you have given up the ghost, everything follows with dead certainty, even in the midst of chaos. From the beginning it was never anything but chaos: it was a fluid which enveloped me, which I breathed in through the gills. In the substrata, where the moon shone steady and opaque, it was smooth and fecundating; above it was a jangle and a discord. In everything I quickly saw the opposite, the contradiction, and between the real and the unreal the irony, the paradox. I was my own worst enemy. There was nothing I wished to do which I could just as well not do. Even as a child, when I lacked for nothing, I wanted to die: I wanted to surrender because I saw no sense in struggling. I felt that nothing would be proved, substantiated, added or subtracted by continuing an existence which I had not asked for. Everybody around me was a failure, or if not a failure, ridiculous. Especially the successful ones. The successful ones bored me to tears. I was sympathetic to a fault, but it was not sympathy that made me so. It was a purely negative quality, a weakness which blossomed at the mere sight of human misery. I never helped any one expecting that it would do any good; I helped because I was helpless to do otherwise. To want to change the condition of affairs seemed futile to me; nothing would be altered, I was convinced, except by a change of heart, and who could change the hearts of men? Now and then a friend was converted: it was something to make me puke. I had no more need of God than He had of me, and if there were one, I often said to myself I would meet Him calmly and spit in His face.

—*Tropic of Capricorn* (1939), Henry Miller

". . . I helped because I was helpless to do otherwise." Once again, as with Huck's heart overcoming his conscience in helping Jim, Miss Watson's property, run off to freedom, the heart is helpless "at the mere sight of human misery." Like Whitman, Miller lifts his barbaric yawp over the rooftops of the world. Unlike Whitman, he sees America as a wasteland where souls dry up with air-conditioning, household goods, cars, work, cleanliness, and righteousness, all the material goods which pave over the live, wet seed in Henry Miller.

Miller's second novel, *Tropic of Capricorn* (or of the goat, a beast famed for lechery), highlights "Val," or Henry Valentine Miller, and begins in time before his first novel, *Tropic of Cancer* (1934). It's something of a bawdy companion to *Plexus* (1953), my favorite Miller novel, a fat, sexless retelling of his Brooklyn childhood and youth at the turn of the century. *Capricorn* is set in Manhattan and luxuriates in sex. Its greatest passages show him hiring and firing for the Cosmodemonic Telegraph Company of North America—he'd been a personnel manager for Western Union for five years in the midtwenties, a job that was: "Chaos! A howling chaos! No need to choose a particular day. Any day of my life—back there— would suit. Every day of my life, my tiny, microcosmic life, was a reflection of the outer chaos."

It's not only his family's Germanic orderliness that Miller explodes in *Capricorn*. He wages, as well, a one-man revolution against American puritanism, the prison of the rules-shackled life he has walked out on. He does this by drawing himself as a lovable rogue and guiltless screwer of hapless women, loading his pages with joyously quivering and vibrating sex, a pulsating flow of four-letter words such as had never before seen ink, and by exploding all the rules of fine writing. The "plot" goes forward, unbuttoned and abandoned, at Miller's whim and is often broken into by surreal arias whose words imitate paint and create a thick paste of impressions squirting from Miller's anarchic spirit. Miller's tongue may be freed but the reader often tires before these arias exhaust themselves, since Miller sees himself as a cosmologist uniting all parts of the universe into one novel-structure. Otherwise, his impulse is to prance like a goat through every paragraph and this certainly infects us, makes us laugh aloud—a laughter that helps fulfill his purpose, to free us from our chains. The writing falls into bogs here and there, but his first paragraph is a near-perfect marvel. Even the surreal metaphor, in which Miller says chaos was a smooth and fecundating fluid in which he breathed through the gills under a jangle and a discord, sets the tone: he will be free to write as he pleases and at an instinctual depth treated this century only by D. H. Lawrence—and by Miller himself four years earlier in *Tropic of Cancer*. One unclear note is the word "converted." At first Miller seems to mean converted by a change of heart, as we think following "who could change the hearts of men?" But he means converted by a clergyman, such as a priest—"it was something to make me puke." In a hymn to chaos such as this stanza, hatred of the clergy is as sunlight to a grape arbor. But Miller forces the puke and spit and their flippancy rounds things out with less strength than he might have mustered. He sounds tinny.

Cancer begins superbly:

> I am living at the Villa Borghese. There is not a crumb of dirt anywhere, nor a chair misplaced. We are all alone here and we are dead.

> Last night Boris discovered that he was lousy. I had to shave his armpits and even then the itching did not stop. How can one get lousy in a place like this? But no matter. We might never have known each other so intimately, Boris and I, had it not been for the lice.
>   —*Tropic of Cancer* (1934), Henry Miller

It's about spiritual rot, with Miller scraping and digging away to let air in on the infections and sores blighting us. In *Capricorn* he peels back the head of his prick and dances in a vat full of vaginas as juicy as grapes. This satyr ignores all in a woman but her pussy. A fully drawn female here would be out of place—but that Miller really can draw a woman in the round is shown in *Plexus*. The same sweeping away of fine-arts writing, the great draft of fresh air through a smokefilled room that *Capricorn* was when it first appeared blows over us again in Holden Caulfield's sneering goddam at fine writing and all that crap. A spring breeze in the stifling fifties.

One fine morning the god Dionysus, feeling fit and joyous and wanting to break something, his skin crawling with an urge to create, went down into Paris, put on a smiling white face mask called "Henry Miller" and wrote the first paragraph of *Tropic of Capricorn*.

Having traced some branchings of Twain's genius, let's see what Carson McCullers is up to:

It happened that green and crazy summer when Frankie was twelve years old. This was the summer when for a long time she had not been a member. She belonged to no club and was a member of nothing in the world. Frankie had become an unjoined person who hung around in doorways, and she was afraid. In June the trees were bright dizzy green, but later the leaves darkened, and the town turned black and shrunken under the glare of the sun. At first Frankie walked around doing one thing and another. The sidewalks of the town were gray in the early morning and at night, but the noon sun put a glaze on them, so that the cement burned and glittered like glass. The sidewalks finally became too hot for Frankie's feet, and also she got herself in trouble. She was in so much secret trouble that she thought it was better to stay at home—and at home there was only Berenice Sadie Brown and John Henry West. The three of them sat at the kitchen table, saying the same things over and over, so that by August the words began to rhyme with each other and sound strange. The world seemed to die each afternoon and nothing moved any longer. At last the summer was like a green sick dream, or like a silent crazy jungle under glass. And then, on the last Friday of August,

all this was changed: it was so sudden that Frankie puzzled the whole blank afternoon, and still she did not understand.
—*The Member of the Wedding* (1946), Carson McCullers

This is sheer heaven, sizzling and limpid, the streets unreeling before Frankie like pictures arising in esters from her own skin or drifting from a small bottle of banana oil or airplane dope. Our skin races and we plunge into a boy/girl as if into a "green sick dream" and bursting hormones prickle our arms.

Among first paragraphs we've looked at so far, only Tolstoy stepped outside himself as a storyteller. McInerney was "You" but we know who that is. When I was much younger, I looked down on the "I" storyteller, at least in the novel. I longed to write huge vivid descriptions, like Thomas Wolfe's—and *he* never used the first person in his novels. But so far we've seen the first person render marvels of excitement, stuff you can't call fine arts and pottery making. Carson McCullers avoids the first person, loves the languorous openings of a storyteller who has eternity to write in. But somehow she gaffs you under the jaw and drags you into her boat as fast as Miller or Twain or Salinger or McInerney.

Now here's a paradisiacal paragraph written with pomegranate juice on coconut meat. How does she do this? Well, *The Member of the Wedding* was long in the womb and written seven times. She didn't just scratch out that opening over the lunch hour. It breathes with Frankie's suffering, it's a great slavering whiff from McCullers' Bakery at dawn, something wonderful is going on inside this book.

But don't McCullers' words look simple? Really, is this distinguished writing? Do acres of grief and chaos stretch out behind it? Let me give you Dr. Don's Rule for Distinguished Writing. It's in the voice. You get a call from a friend, you know right away who it is. One paragraph, you know the voice. But . . . does this voice show up full-blown in the first draft? Ah ha ha.

Stillborn writing wraps us in long bolts rich with writerly clauses and purple colons and semicolonnic breathstops that no friend still sober would say to us on the phone, nor do the sublime musings of Sir Thomas Browne, his rhetoric in full cry and marching down the page, promise an ideal voice for the storyteller bent on keeping our fingers from the lamp switch. Even Proust, at his most Proustian, *talks* to us. We *know* his voice long before he clears his throat to go on. But maybe these are dumb warnings, nobody writes cloth-of-gold anymore—aside from a few crusty egoists who have a tough time seeing ink, and when they do, get either praised as oracles or whipped like bad dogs. What's not dumb is to fear rereading yourself five years later and finding there's no you in the lines. We spend much of our lives shaping words any wordsmith could have shaped, words voiceless on the page. A sentence must have your voice in it, or forget it. Don't write it! Take eight first paragraphs from page one of *The New York Times*, from the *The New York Times Magazine*, or even *The New York Times Book Review*,* and you hear voices sounding all the

* Here is the First Paragraph of Joyce Carol Oates's review of John Updike's *Rabbit at Rest*:

> With this elegiac volume, John Updike's much-acclaimed and, in retrospect, hugely ambitious Rabbit quartet—"Rabbit, Run" (1960), "Rabbit Redux" (1971), "Rabbit Is Rich" (1981) and now "Rabbit at Rest"—comes to an end. The final word of so many thousands is Rabbit's, and it is, singularly, "Enough." This is, in its context, in an intensive cardiac care unit in a Florida hospital, a judgment both blunt and touchingly modest, valedictory and yet enigmatic. As Rabbit's doctor has informed his wife, "Sometimes it's time." But in the nightmare efficiency of late 20th-century medical technology, in which mere vegetative existence may be defined as life, we are no longer granted such certainty.
> —*The New York Times Book Review*, September 30, 1990

This is Oates writing on Academic Pilot, her voice pitched at Impersonal, the tones of some nameless hack reading prepared notes to a classroom, in a review that stuffs Updike like an owl. As with most *Times* reviews, the reader is forcefed facts until his brain chokes and arms turn to pasta and he knows he's into his Sunday Stupids. Oates is not about her usual writerly writing here but has slipped on a face-saving stiffness for page one of the *Book Review*, should she trip on her own ankles while reviewing a fashionable stylist who is himself a very fancy reviewer. The *Times*, same. Bookchat with a dreadful lack of ballsiness, reporters invisible despite bylines. Do you want to wake up thirty years later facing a shelf of voiceless grist with your name on the covers?

But turning from oblivion, I don't doubt that McCullers's first stanza gave a thin, weak cry when she sang it over months later in light of her growing story. Even the firehose first paragraph of *Tropic of Capricorn* is studied work, much revised. Genius or not, no writer in this book struck off a perfect opening at first try. Photocopies of Miller's typed pages show heavy cutting and are tattooed with second thoughts, as are printer's drafts inked over by Tolstoy and Dostoevsky, who slashed pages, gutted paragraphs and scratched in revisions right up to deadline. So you're not alone when you ball up your first page and tell your wife or husband when she or he brings it back to you, "THIS DON'T SING!"

Much revision takes place unconsciously and we remake our work to fit a pattern not seen by us. All our characters are pieces of us and, in *The Member of the Wedding*, all are pieces of Frankie as well. Berenice's blue glass eye, so ill-matched to her brown eye, echoes Frankie's big splitting off from being a crew cut tomboy in a baseball cap to being a member of the wedding in an orange satin evening dress. The loss of her best friend, six-year-old John Henry, who dies in horrible pain from meningitis, also speeds the fall of the boy side of her boy/girl being. All this happens at a psychic level the author may not be aware of. We have to trust our deeper selves to do this work for us, much as Giotto trusts his hand and wrist in drawing a perfect circle. In fact, the more conscious we are of

I'm sure, was happy with her spacefiller and its note that where in his novel *Couples* (1968) "John Updike explored the human body as Eros, he now explores the body, in yet more detail, as Thanatos." Unh! Here's straw for stuffing a headpiece, the sound of rats' feet over broken glass. So, I get no joy from reading Oates's first paragraph, I had to read it twice for its sense, and any high purpose in it seems merely adopted for the task at hand. Nothing in it springs from inner need or grips me with moral force.

symbols the less their power. Every *thing* or happening in the story must arise from a natural impulse and have a life of its own before it's a symbol, or else it's just a bit of tin rhetoric. Forcing life into a symbol is like making a zombie walk. McCullers's writing breathes forth psychic symbols that happen in the natural course of her storytelling and energize her first paragraph, which jumps with imaginative charges.

Her first paragraph aims to disarm us with delight and lead us into a mystic state. We are going to a wedding of Frankie's two natures into one being.

Now, this is just me. I could write quite different ideas than I have about each of these first paragraphs. If it sounds good, you can write anything you want to write about writing. What depths and hidden criminal impulses Thomas Mann might have found in all these first paragraphs. Frankie, in fact, sees herself as a criminal, which accounts for much of her simmering hysterics, and Huck is self-condemned as a criminal, and "You" is a dope fiend. We could as well be digging away at dark forces as looking for the energies of awakening. But let's stick to what we're doing. I trust my deeper self to lead us to a psychic place where each first paragraph lights up our theme of joyous beginnings even more strongly than we've seen so far. We've just set sail! It's only dawn. And there on the shore sit Tolstoy, Twain, Salinger, McInerney, Miller and McCullers, who've told us by their works how they implored heaven to keep their throats clear for an inspired opening.

Each writer so far is an original who shows us that we must trust ourselves to be ourselves alone and not fall into imitation. I think writers always write never less than their best. Even doing a screenplay, a mystery or western, article, short story or novel, a writer never gives less than his or her best. William Butler Yeats thought there were some things, like journalism, a poet should never do. But then Yeats's clotted richness in his autobiographies could use some sand and loosening up. This leads to my distrust of fine-arts writing in fiction. The writer writing at the top of his form but giving us a neatly metaphored piece of scene-setting in which not a grassblade is untrimmed or uneven—a wordsmith's wonder. The writer models away and when perfection is clearly at hand the paragraph is sent off to the foundry and cast in bronze for eternity to do with as it will. Shakespeare's sonnets make much of this. Me, I want passion, something wild, not perfection's high gloss. Screw good taste, just drop your shirt and show me your scars. Alarm me—because only then will a paragraph you write still be yours when you look at it ten years from now—be something only you could have written! Tell me about your shoplifting. Show me your can of Mace—Christ, what's in that stuff? Forget grandmother's shawl, her armchair doilies and the crocheted motto framed on the wall—unless there's a passion behind them pressing to implode and blow us away. Most amusing for me is McCullers's three-handed bridge game which Frankie, Berenice and John Henry play without knowing they don't have a full deck. Ah, God, did You do that to us? McCullers asks about those missing cards from the first paragraph onward. She knows they're missing from every hand we're dealt and the irony lifts her like a shot of dope.

I'll open up, she says. You want to know about losses, and what's missing, and what's hoped for? Well, I'll tell you . . . but in a green sick dream.

Virginia Woolf would follow a novel that taxed her genius to the full, and often excited her nearly to madness, with a less tiring work she thought of more as a lark. *A Room of One's Own*, her book-length essay on women writers, helped her settle down from the great burst of sustained imagination that carried her through *To the Lighthouse*. I want to talk about both masterpieces and will start with the essay.

But, you may say, we asked you to speak about women and fiction—what has that got to do with a room of one's own? I will try to explain. When you asked me to speak about women and fiction I sat down on the banks of a river and began to wonder what the words meant. They might mean simply a few remarks about Fanny Burney; a few more about Jane Austen; a tribute to the Brontës and a sketch of Haworth Parsonage under snow; some witticisms if possible about Miss Mitford; a respectful allusion to George Eliot; a reference to Mrs. Gaskell and one would have done. But at second sight the words seemed not so simple. The title woman and fiction might mean, and you may have meant it to mean, women and what they are like; or it might mean women and the fiction that they write; or it might mean women and the fiction that is written about them; or it might mean that somehow all three are inextricably mixed together and you want me to consider them in that light. But when I began to consider the subject in this last way, which seemed the most interesting, I soon saw that it had one fatal drawback. I should never be able to come to a conclusion. I should never be able to fulfil what is, I understand, the first duty of a lecturer—to hand you after an hour's discourse a nugget of pure truth to wrap up between the pages of your notebooks and keep on the mantel-piece for ever. All I could do was to offer you an opinion upon one minor point—a woman must have money and a room of her own if she is to write fiction; and that, as you will see, leaves the great problem of the true nature of woman and the true nature of fiction unsolved. I have shirked the duty of coming to a conclusion upon these two questions—women and fiction remain, so far as I am concerned, unsolved problems. But in order to make some amends I am going to do what I can to show you how I arrived at this opinion about the room and the money. I am going to develop in your presence as fully and freely as I can the train of thought which led me to think this. Perhaps if I lay bare the ideas, the prejudices, that lie behind this statement you will find that they have some bearing upon women and some upon fiction. At any rate, when a subject is highly controversial—and any question about sex is that—one cannot hope to tell the truth. One can only show how one came to hold whatever opinion one does hold. One can only give one's audience the chance of drawing their own conclusions as they observe the limitations, the prejudices, the idiosyncrasies of the speaker. Fiction here is likely to contain more truth than fact. Therefore I propose, making use of all the liberties and licences of a novelist, to tell you the story of the two days that preceded my coming here—how, bowed down by the weight of the subject which you have laid upon my shoulders, I pondered it, and made it work in and out of my daily life. I need not say that what I am about to describe has no existence: Oxbridge is an invention; so is Fernham; "I" is only a convenient term for somebody who has no real being. Lies will flow from my lips, but there may perhaps be some truth mixed up with them; it is for you to seek out this truth and to decide whether any part of it is worth keeping. If not, you will of course throw the whole of it into the wastepaper basket and forget all about it.

—*A Room of One's Own* (1929), Virginia Woolf

Despite everything she tells us, I thought for many years that this imaginary essay was a talk Woolf gave at "Oxbridge" and later filled out for book publication! It's actually a rewrite and fusion of two talks she gave. But for me it's as much for an imagined audience as Kafka's wonderful "A Report to the Academy" in which an ape gives an after-dinner talk about its learning years at the Academy.

It all sounds so reserved, right? But Woolf is not long underway before we hear the far-off screams of a prisoner in her cell, first in the way she tries to make sense of the idiotic topic she's been asked to speak on, then in the mocking way she strings together but rapidly dismisses some important English women writers, whom she now sees as really no help in putting together a suitable academic banality about women who write. Later in the essay we find that the charming riverbank she sat on to think over her topic is off limits to women, who must keep to the gravel paths, and is for male students only—a bit of broken glass she buries in her third sentence for us to step on later. Woolf speaks mildly but is ready to break bones about being a second-sex writer. I say mildly, but her restraint is superhuman. She knows that any show of anger or bitterness will only prejudice her case and enforce things as they are. So she adopts a tone of polite reason and fairness while running a psychic knife through our ribs.

In five stages of argument she undermines male pride as first-sex writers, makes clear the unfair state women are in, sketches what's needed, and delivers her whole work with immense passion and without a single harsh word. She's clear-spoken throughout. She infects us with her theme. Her whole being is behind every word. She brings such genius to her case against man's inhumanity to woman that we are won over equally by her vast ease with words as by the rightness of her cause. At first it sounds laughable: "A woman must have money and a room of her own if she is to write fiction." Instantly, I feel anguish. *She* needs a room and some money to write fiction? Who doesn't! That's not just a woman's problem. But Woolf makes it stick, that women writers are poorer than men in so many ways that they are a special case.

Woolf carries her argument even into grammar, that women need their own *sentence*. "The weight, the pace, the stride of a man's mind are too unlike her own. . . ." Man's sentence is too clumsy for woman, she must strain to fill out its rhythms. "Jane Austen looked at it and laughed at it and devised a perfectly natural, shapely sentence proper for her own use and never departed from it." Woolf thinks the epic and the poetic play just as unsuitable as the striding sentence. "Moreover, a book is not made of sentences laid end to end, but of sentences built, if an image helps, into arcades or domes. And this shape too has been made by men out of their own needs for their own uses." By the time woman became a writer "all the older forms of literature were hardened and set. . . ." She's serious—these arguments are not literary burlesque. I've just gone back through the essay looking for a sentence—her idea haunts me—full of "those unsaid or half-said words" or words "in the shortest of shorthand, in words that are hardly syllabled yet" that might be thought pure Woolf in beat or womanly rhythms, something "all half lights and profound shadows like those serpentine caves where one goes with a candle peering up and down, not knowing where one is stepping"—but I couldn't find it.

"Yes, of course, if it's fine tomorrow," said Mrs. Ramsay. "But you'll have to be up with the lark," she added.

To her son these words conveyed an extraordinary joy, as if it were settled, the expedition were bound to take place, and the wonder to which he had looked forward, for years and years it seemed, was, after a night's darkness and a day's sail, within touch. Since he belonged, even at the age of six, to that great clan which cannot keep this feeling separate from that, but must let future prospects, with their joys and sorrows, cloud what is actually at hand, since to such people even in earliest childhood any turn in the wheel of sensation has the power to crystallise and transfix the moment upon which its gloom or radiance rests, James Ramsay, sitting on the floor cutting out pictures from the illustrated catalogue of the Army and Navy Stores, endowed the picture of a refrigerator, as his mother spoke, with heavenly bliss. It was fringed with joy. The wheelbarrow, the lawnmower, the sound of poplar trees, leaves whitening before rain, rooks cawing, brooms knocking, dresses rustling—all these were so coloured and distinguished in his mind that he had already his private code, his secret language, though he appeared the image of stark and uncompromising severity, with his high forehead and his fierce blue eyes, impeccably candid and pure, frowning slightly at the sight of human frailty, so that his mother, watching him guide his scissors neatly round the refrigerator, imagined him all red and ermine on the Bench or directing a stern and momentous enterprise in some crisis of public affairs.

"But," said his father, stopping in front of the drawing-room window, "it won't be fine."

—*To the Lighthouse* (1927), Virginia Woolf

No, I couldn't find that pure Woolfian sentence in *A Room of One's Own*—but this is a mother lode, with the reader peering around a candleflame in a cave trying to follow the serpentine path of what's happening. *To the Lighthouse* is no novel for skimmers of dull parts, since it is *all* dull parts—unless, of course, you read like a poet and weigh every syllable for gold. Yes, it's dense. But notice that there's not one ornament dangling anywhere. This is not a description of grandmother's doilies—it's perfervid, and only gets more so, and takes place just where Woolf said she wanted her novels to take place, down underground in a secret language, with psychic waves flowing between bliss-bestowing Mrs. Ramsay and six-year-old James with "his fierce blue eyes, impeccably candid and pure," and spoilsport Mr. Ramsay.

Intense stuff! And the next sentence is even more so: "Had there been an axe handy, or a poker, any weapon that would have gashed a hole in his father's breast and killed him, there and then, James would have seized it." That's so satisfying. Not what the unwary expect from a six-year-old—but James is his father's greatest rival among the Ramsay's eight children.

Woolf sees the Ramsays as a psychic system and never gives us a journalistic fact about them—no journalism in Woolf! As she says in a letter in 1941, after an illness: "Oh yes, I can write: I mean I've a fizz of ideas. What I dread is bottling them to order." Everything in *To the Lighthouse* takes place under a running stream, broken tempers among adults, soothings, grinding tensions, even the children's horseplay, and—off-stage—three deaths. In the Woolfian novel's new womanly view of history, great events happen in households, not in the bloodlettings of World War One. Mrs. Ramsay is the centerpost while ever-eruptive Mr. Ramsay, once a leading philosopher but now deadrot within, keeps an ever more stern shell of seeming command. The children detest his sternness, the empty shouts of verse with which he girds himself, his blue-sky bolts of temper. A bug in his soup can dynamite the dinner table. Yet it is Mrs. Ramsay, who has flaws but also divine intuition, from whom all strength flows, as in this sentence from a dinner scene:

> . . . Now she need not listen. It could not last, she knew, but at the moment her eyes were so clear that they seemed to go round the table unveiling each of these people, and their thoughts and their feelings, without effort like a light stealing under water so that its ripples and the reeds in it and the minnows balancing themselves, and the sudden silent trout are lit up hanging, trembling.

In writing about her family, Woolf is herself each member, becoming the milk-giving mother, the ironfisted but stupefyingly self-pitying father, and all her brothers and sisters, particularly James, who wants to gash in his father's chest. She writes ten years after her father's death, but only in becoming each member can Woolf the woman see each of her parts clearly ("the minnows balancing themselves"). With the heat of a poet's eye and the need to break down old forms and boldly make a new novel equal to her artistic passions, she holds herself whole ("hanging, trembling"), cured for the moment of the madness that at last did drive her to death by drowning—for she walked into the River Ouse with her pockets filled with stones.

I don't say these things with any authority as an analyst, only as a reader and fellow writer who understands the emotional purges and healing nature of novel-writing. With each work the novelist lays to rest great tracts of inner disquiet, a restlessness that has little or no further power over her. All this soulworking appears full-blown in James's bliss in the first paragraph, a bliss flooding from a refrigerator in a catalogue but invested into James's yearning to sail in a small boat to the almost mythic lighthouse a few miles offshore from the family's summer cottage. James makes the journey only as a lad of seventeen, after the war, and it is a discomforting trip—with James now at the tiller and sheets—that in no way uplifts him or rekindles his bliss, but only brings him heavily down to earth. Woolf, too, makes the trip, her family ghosts now earthbound, pricked of their mythic power and no longer able to hurt her. Upon reaching the lighthouse, Mr. Ramsay leaps ashore, in sudden triumph, praising James's seasmanship. After this novel Woolf never looks back. She has reached the lighthouse in completing this novel and earned her late father's psychic praise at having given birth to a new idea in art, something he'd coveted in philosophy but failed to achieve. She has triumphed, won mental balance for now by trial of artistry.

William Kennedy's *Ironweed* takes place in the demonic underworld of Francis Phelan, at a depth of soul not too distant from that of *To the Lighthouse* and struck instantly in the first paragraph:

> Riding up the winding road of Saint Agnes Cemetery in the back of the rattling old truck, Francis Phelan became aware that the dead, even more than the living, settled down in neighborhoods. The truck was suddenly surrounded by fields of monuments and cenotaphs of kindred design and striking size, all guarding the privileged dead. But the truck moved on and the limits of mere privilege became visible, for here now came the acres of truly prestigious death: illustrious men and women, captains of life without their diamonds, furs, carriages, and limousines, but buried in pomp and glory, vaulted in great tombs built like heavenly safe deposit boxes, or parts of the Acropolis. And ah yes, here too, inevitably, came the flowing masses, row upon row of them

under simple headstones and simpler crosses. Here was the neighborhood of the Phelans.

—*Ironweed* (1983), William Kennedy

This paragraph's high purpose and manner of statement is a variation on the noble Augustan march of Samuel Johnson's prose and the theme of his great poem "On the Vanity of Human Wishes," as well as on the theme of Sir Thomas Browne's great essay "Hydrotaphia, or Urn-Burial". From high seriousness Kennedy veers into sheer novelty when the next paragraph shows us dead Phelans alive and grumbling in their graves, with the mother twitching nervously and eating dead dandelions and weeds that give her ghost-stomach waves of nausea, the father smoking dried roots of grass he grinds to dust in his fingers and packs into his pipe. Do we want to go along with this strange, almost mocking, stuff about buried Phelans? Slowly we accept this graveyard's laws, for this is Francis's real world, the Irish Catholic's limbo, a stage of the afterlife. These living dead hold in their auras the deepest values of Francis's life, laws he still measures himself by, and yet these are dreamfolk of his hallucinating alcoholic brain.

Francis, a once-heroic ballplayer who has slaughtered two men and, after only a couple of beers, accidentally killed his own baby Gerald by letting him slip from his diaper and fall to the floor, has been paying for his sins for twenty-two years on the bum. Saul Bellow writes a skillful thumbnail of Francis which can hardly be bettered and is worth quoting, despite coming from the novel's dust jacket: "Francis is also a traditional champion, the fated man, a type out of Icelandic or Irish epic. To kill is his destiny, and he kills American style, with techniques learned in play, throwing a rock like a baseball and, again in Hooverville, hitting a man with a baseball bat. He considers himself a man of sin."

Again and again in *Ironweed*, Kennedy's power to bring light into dark places and to write tragic dialogue ringing with a Shakespearean blackness strikes me as the happiest art. I have a fellow writer who calls this phantasmal dead-baby stuff corn. But for me it's bliss, as when Francis prays above Gerald:

> In his grave, a cruciformed circle, Gerald watched the advent of his father . . . Gerald's grave trembled with superb possibility. Denied speech in life, having died with only monosyllabic goos and gaahs in his vocabulary, Gerald possessed the gift of tongues in death. His ability to communicate and to understand was at the genius level among the dead. He could speak with any resident adult in any language, but more notable was his ability to understand the chattery squirrels and chipmunks, the silent signals of the ants and beetles, and the slithy semaphores of the slugs and worms that moved above and through his earth. He could read the waning flow of energy in the leaves and berries as they fell from the box elder above him. . . . His body had not only been absolved of the need to decay, but in some respects—a full head of hair, for instance—it had grown to a completeness that was both natural and miraculous. Gerald rested in infantile sublimity, exuding a high gloss induced by early death, his skin a radiant white-gold, his nails a silvery gray, his cluster of curls and large eyes perfectly matched in gleaming ebony. . . . He was neither beautiful nor perfect to the beholder but rather an ineffably fabulous presence whose like was not to be found anywhere in the cemetery, and it abounded with dead innocents.

In this reader's heart, Kennedy will have a hard time getting upriver of his success in *Ironweed*. And yet, as we said about McInerney's success in *Bright Lights, Big City*, and Fitzgerald's in *The Great Gatsby*, authors must not be asked to repeat perfect works. One tour de force in a career—all stops pulled on his mighty Wurlitzer and every phrase shaped to his fingering—is enough. Could Dickens match himself with a second *A Christmas Carol*?

What is so attractive about Kennedy's voice in this opening paragraph? Perhaps it's the subject matter—the social grid Kennedy finds in the fields of death, his ironies hitting bulls-eyes phrase after phrase—as much as his way of speaking. First we are taken in by Francis's sense of the gravestones falling into neighborhoods, with monuments and cenotaphs marching by in noble Latin, and then Kennedy undercuts the illustrious dead with an amused commonplace, that they are vaulted in "heavenly safe deposit boxes. . . ." Then irony fades before "the flowing masses, row upon row of them under simple headstones and simpler crosses. Here was the neighborhood of the Phelans." No granite Latin diction for the Phelans.

So the author's voice follows an arc, rises from the rattling old truck to the august and glorious, spreads to acres of the illustrious, then falls to the familiar and sweepingly sad. These "flowing masses" and Kennedy's black Irish wit disarm and move us. I, for one, enter the heaven of a writer absolutely on top of his material from the first sound of his voice. Please, none of that moldiness that writing's all work and slavery. His undercurrent of unkillable laughter that carries us safely through sudden upwelling sadness: Can that come from a mere factifying stonemason and bricklayer of words sweating under a fluorescent desk lamp? Mr. Kennedy's no hod carrier. His load is light, every page. Pure light. And surely he changes our lives, enriches our understanding of the madness of one drunk in a fellowship of rock-bottom boozers during the Great Depression. It's not just historical understanding he gives us. We become Francis Phelan, a deep-witted walking grave, lighted up with family ghosts like fireflies in twilight.

> "Hey, bum" he called to Rudy. "Let's find that truck driver."
>
> "Whattayou been up to?" Rudy asked. "You know somebody buried up there?"
>
> "A little kid I used to know."
>
> "A kid? What'd he do, die young?"

"Pretty young."

"What happened to him?"

"He fell."

"He fell where?"

"He fell on the floor."

"Hell, I fall on the floor about twice a day and I ain't dead."

"That's what you think," Francis said.

Here is another Francis, this one Flannery O'Connor's, and a Protestant, or anti-Protestant, Southerner (though O'Connor herself was a Catholic):

> Francis Marion Tarwater's uncle had been dead for only half a day when the boy got too drunk to finish digging his grave and a Negro named Buford Munson, who had come to get a jug filled, had to finish it and drag the body from the breakfast table where it was still sitting and bury it in a decent and Christian way, with the sign of its Saviour at the head of the grave and enough dirt on top to keep the dogs from digging it up. Buford had come along about noon and when he left at sundown, the boy, Tarwater, had never returned from the still.
>
> —*The Violent Bear It Away* (1960), Flannery O'Connor

The shortest of O'Connor's novels, here is a matchlessly intense artistic success which shows how religious mania grips three members of a Southern family, and how two of them fight it as if they are slinging rocks at Jesus with intent to maim first and then kill. These two spit on the Resurrection and see Judgment Day as a nauseous sucker's game. Despite that, they've been so deep-dyed with the Christian belief they reject that one goes mad and splits off an alter ego who orders him about, and the other walks a thin line between unreality and emptiness, hoping that at his death he'll have the strength to throw himself into the emptiness rather than into the falsity of the Christian afterlife. Hard to follow? These crazed folks are seen with a photographic exactness of their inner states equal to newsreels of the *Hindenburg* falling in fire like some Nazi Lucifer. But nearly to the end, O'Connor's wit lightens the story's grimness.

The first paragraph tells us something that the main character, fourteen-year-old Francis Marion Tarwater, called Tarwater, doesn't know because he was drunk when it happened, that a Negro neighbor gave Tarwater's uncle Mason a Christian burial. Tarwater, when he sobers up on the night of his great-uncle's death, thinks his aged uncle still sits indoors at the breakfast table where he died. So Tarwater, rather than bury the old fanatic, whom he despises, burns the house down around him. The uncle has again and again told Tarwater he wants a Christian burial and not to be cremated. Tarwater now believes that burning up his uncle's body has freed him from the old man's baleful eyes. Although his mind rejects his uncle, with whom he has lived alone in the Tennessee backwoods almost since birth, every word he speaks comes from the sword-edge of his uncle's teachings. He has no other wordbag to speak with as he marches off to the city to prove to himself and his late uncle that he is *not* the fire-tongued prophet that his uncle raised him to be. But, as he finds, his uncle is not cremated but lies hungering under a wooden cross in Tarwater's brainpaths, awaiting the Resurrection and a lunch of multiplied loaves and fishes with Jesus. Tarwater, with wondrous scorn and rationality (learned from uncle Mason), makes clear to George Rayber, his foster father in the city, that schoolteacher George's city-taught, dried out grip on reality is shoddy and that George's battle against his upbringing by uncle Mason is lost utterly. Tarwater's sense of reality is beyond arguing: there is no Jesus, no Resurrection, the Children of God die like hogs, and the only difference between people and hogs is that people can "calculate."

The first paragraph sets the practical tone with which Southerners accept bizarre beliefs. As a truckdriver who gives Tarwater a lift mutters, "You belong in the booby hatch. . . . You ride through these states and you see they all belong in it. I won't see nobody sane again until I get back to Detroit." O'Connor's irony throughout sides with the truckdriver, but her novelist's heart allows her to stretch out on a bed of rock salt in her characters' most hidden places and listen to their ravings with the heart of an angel.

Sympathy with her characters inspires her everywhere. She has a fine brush for peacock-colored landscape and wheels of Christian fire, a tuning-fork ear for Southern talk and Tarwater's "going about my bidness," but her genius is for becoming one with every character on her page. She does it so well that her art nowhere shows the effort by which she steals through them like brookwater and speaks the heartsound behind every stony-eyed glint, the unsaid word cramped behind each mouth. When Tarwater tells Rayber, who wears a hearing aid, how he burned up their uncle Mason, "Rayber heard his own heart, magnified by the hearing aid, suddenly begin to pound like the works of a gigantic machine in his chest." But O'Connor hears into every chest, without a hearing aid.

Do I rhapsodize? Well, why not? This twilight where the writer lifts out of herself, seeks backward through memory for her lost heart and sees each weed in her path as "a live green nerve" (O'Connor) is where I feel at one with Durer painting his self-portrait or a great piece of turf in heaven, Mahler sending up fiddles for Alma, Bach playing the organ for the greater glory of God, Kafka chasing shadows in Prague, Rilke in his astral rose garden. Do you think writers of these first paragraphs are on forced marches toward some wretched deadline? Dickens was, perhaps, as we'll see, but only for his first drafts. When it comes time for reprinting his magazine serials in hard covers, he opens his third eye and awaits the wingbeat of his angel. Unlike the journalist with his facts before him, his card file, telephone and reference works, these midnight storytellers—their Muse deep in pearl cloud and just glinting on the nightsea—have only their intuition and desire to excel as compasses over waves of feeling, with their charged first paragraph at hand as a touchstone for courage. Quite often each makes landfall on a morning or afternoon not foreseen and unexpectedly writes his last paragraph, sits back amazed, looks up with wild hope that his vision's fulfilled. Soon enough his first draft turns to cheesecloth. Now comes the gut-magic of making the dumb page speak, an entirely different magic from the wrenchings that got the first draft joined together. That befogged, misbegotten draft, it turns out, was all heart, no head. Now for shaping, for breaking off thick crusts of fine writing, packing light into groping characterizations, those places where faith pushed on through blind hours that only weeks or months later can be made to glow. The second draft ends. But now comes a need for mastery of the story's events, a sense of the author looking down in judgment. This is a still different kind of writing, a merciless shearing, trimming, hard sewing that changes mere woolliness and fleece into an author's robe, bearing a certain pride in the cut. And yet now comes the hard part, the final revision for voice, for pitching each word at the same beat of high purpose and expectation as the first paragraph. Should I cut this paragraph about the storyteller's courage, the revisions that change Frankenstein's monster into Prometheus? Should I cut that last sentence? No one can force life into a dead limb. It's best to cut, not just scrape. My surgical saw lifts, moves to the head of the sentence, waves over the whole passage . . . but with a last breath, I invoke my first paragraph. Is this chitchat or did I write it on Olympus? Something organic, or two-headed? Is that green glow health or gangrene? Only the voice can tell us, and so we read it aloud. Does it breathe? If it breathes, it may well be alive. And even if alive, the whole may have years of mellowing ahead, since works written in heaven don't always find an earthly outlet during their author's lifetime. This means only that the author had the great pleasure of fathering them, sharing them with his mate and close friends, and the unequaled satisfaction of carrying the rich light in his children's eyes to the grave with him unstained by publishers' losses. Their feelings will never go out of fashion, their perfect limbs fade from the shelf. A work of heart that dies in the stores is as painful to think about as one that never sees printer's ink, there's hardly any difference in the agony. The fun of writing is in feelings and joining feelings to a larger feeling. Publishing is like the door on the madhouse being thrown open for two weeks every few years, you go wandering around the countryside through book stores, and then all the reviews are in, publication day is quite dead, and it's back to dreamland. Sometimes the door doesn't open, pub day doesn't happen, you get sick at the thought of book stores, and so you dream, with your hair somewhat whiter, about your child in the trunk finding future ink. Stone-cold revision a year or two later may suck out fatty passages and give bloom to others, but you may have to settle for the long view, of being read in heaven. At least the child that yearned to be born is written and not just some speechless thing in your chest. Its eternal life is not in your hands. You wrote in your dreams. What more can you ask of Paradise?

Some readers may think Alice Walker's *The Color Purple* was written out of social purpose. But stories are written to be loved. Those written for social purpose die fastest, though the novel of ideas has a dead man's lope of its own. You can wave goodbye to both at their first ads in the *Sunday Times*. *The Color Purple* is a book to be loved forever, not as a landmark in a social movement to free a people and a sex in bondage, but as a marvel of imagination in which an author is invaded by voices that take on grubby, dung-beetle lives of their own but later became beautiful scarab-backed creatures. Like prophets who plant their staffs and let the Wind speak through them, Walker plants her pen and lets all in bondage speak through her:

You better not never tell nobody but God. It'd kill your mammy.
Dear God,

I am fourteen years old. **I am** I have always been a good
girl. Maybe you can give me a sign letting me know what is
happening to me.

Last spring after little Lucious come I hear them fussing.
He was pulling on her arm. She say It too soon, Fonso, I
ain't well. Finally he leave her alone. A week go by, he
pulling on her arm again. She say Naw, I ain't gonna. Can't
you see I'm already half dead, an all of these children.

She went to visit her sister doctor over Macon. Left me
to see after the others. He never had a kine word to say to
me. Just say You gonna do what your mammy wouldn't.
First he put his thing up gainst hip and sort of wiggle it
around. Then he grab hold my titties. Then he push his
thing inside my pussy. When that hurt, I cry. He start to
choke me, saying You beter shut up and git used to it.

But I don't never git used to it. And now I feels sick
every time I be the one to cook. My mama she fuss at me
an look at me. She happy, cause he good to her now. But
too sick to last long.

—*The Color Purple* (1982), Alice Walker

Both Alice Walker and Mark Twain stride into their
novels with storytellers who are disappointed in life and
mankind and speaking a Southern lingo. Huck sees dishon-
esty everywhere, is beaten and nearly murdered by his Pap.
Walker's Celie is raped many times by a man she thinks is
her father and bears him two children. Somehow Huck
and Celie's disappointment, a sense of mankind as damned,
binds them with ties of love to fellow outcasts and to the
supernal glory of nature. Society itself is not to be borne.
Huck's horror is offset by his tie with Jim, which passes
through a crucible of conscience, and by a kind of moral
reading of nature as he lies naked on his raft under the night
stars, or watches a rising storm:

. . . Pretty soon it darkened up and begun to thunder and lighten; so the birds was right about it. Directly it begun to rain, and it rained like all fury, too, and I never see the wind blow so. It was one of these regular summer storms. It would get so dark that it looked all blue-black outside, and lovely; and the rain would thrash along by so thick that the trees off a little ways looked dim and spider-webby; and here would come a blast of wind that would bend the trees down and turn up the pale underside of the leaves; and then a perfect ripper of a gust would follow along and set the branches to tossing their arms as if they was just wild; and next, when it was just about the bluest and blackest—*fst!* it was as bright as glory and you'd have a little glimpse of tree-tops a-plunging about, away off yonder in the storm, hundreds of yards further than you could see before; dark as sin again in a second, and now you'd hear the thunder let go with an awful crash and then go rumbling, grumbling, tumbling down the sky towards the under side of the world, like rolling empty barrels down stairs, where it's long stairs and they bounce a good deal, you know.

He sees the storm's height as *bright as glory*, a Christian phrase that shows us his mind strikingly well, and the storm's depths as *dark as sin*. Twain makes sure that what would otherwise be a pictorial setpiece that stops the story's flow is anchored in character and not just rapturous warbling. Celie's disasters are also offset by love, for her far-off sister in Africa, for her bisexual lover, the beautiful Shug (for Sugar) Avery, and by Shug's awakening her to God in nature:

. . . Listen, God love everything you love—and a mess of stuff you don't. But more than anything, God love admiration.

You saying God vain, I ast.

Naw, she say. Not vain, just wanting to share a good

thing. I think it pisses God off if you walk by the color purple in a field somewhere and don't notice it.

This is a novel of lasting worth. Hemingway said, in *Green Hills of Africa*, "Dostoevsky was made by being sent to Siberia. Writers are forged in injustice as a sword is forged." Alice Walker was forged as a witness to the all-encircling chains the Southern black woman was born into following Emancipation up through the twenties and thirties.

As with Virginia Woolf's *A Room of One's Own*, her language is pitched at an eloquence all the more savage for its restraint. There is barely a lyrical moment and yet the style sings and the misspelling takes on a music of its own. The story is told through letters, some to God, some to Celie's sister, some *from* her sister telling about blacks in Africa. No letter is ever answered, but the act of letter-writing cramps us painfully with Celie's heart-squeezings. If God has any answers they come from Shug Avery as love, acceptance, practical advice, and Celie's emotional education. Celie plasters over all her feelings, though the reader sees them, as in the paragraphs above. Only Shug can unbind Celie's heart and let her see herself plainly.

That Walker, like Woolf, is engaged in freeing women from sexual bondage in no way makes this a political novel any more than Woolf's essay is a political pamphlet. The men in both works condemn themselves by their minds and actions. Outright attacks on them would not help, only make the reader carp. Woolf and Walker are too smart to raise their voices. Where Woolf vividly brings up a writer's agony in not having a room to write in, Walker brings up the agony the country black woman has in not having a decent place to put her two feet, much less sit down and write. Celie's life shrinks into a nutshell. The novel takes us through the cracking of that shell and toward serenity thirty years hence, *her* Independence Day.

41

The novel's paradisiacal quality for me comes in Walker's endowing a thirty-year period before her birth with funky, lived-in memory. This is a writer's dream, to stretch one's sensibilities and walk the earth of another era in search of a people for whom one has blood-feelings, and then to walk there each writing day, all yearning fulfilled. That's a homecoming to dip into, a cabin to sit in and scratch out a first paragraph in the voice of someone living there and then.

> Through the bloody September twilight, aftermath of sixty-two rainless days, it had gone like a fire in dry grass—the rumor, the story, whatever it was. Something about Miss Minnie Cooper and a Negro. Attacked, insulted, frightened: none of them, gathered in the barber shop on that Saturday evening where the ceiling fan stirred, without freshening it, the vitiated air, sending back upon them, in recurrent surges of stale pomade and lotion, their own stale breath and odors, knew exactly what had happened.
>
> —"Dry September" (1931), *Collected Stories*, William Faulkner

This great opening—a fire spreading suddenly and everywhere through a field—rushes us instantly into its world by lynching its grammar. Is this slipshod or artful writing? We'll never know. Since Faulkner magnificently achieves his desired effects, does grammar matter? Isn't a hanging of sense the subject? Isn't *hanging*?

The paragraph opens like wildfire: I see a huge blood-red sun at earth's edge, and the rumor, the sentence bursts over me, through me, whatever. "Something about Miss Minnie Cooper and a Negro. Attacked, insulted, frightened: . . . ." Who is attacked? Miss Minnie? The Negro? No, attacked, insulted and frightened are some men gathered in a barber shop. ". . . gathered in the barber shop on that Saturday evening where the ceiling fan stirred. . . ." What, what? Surely he means *when?* No, it's "that Saturday evening where the ceiling fan stirred, without freshening it. . . ." What, without freshening the Saturday evening? without freshening the fan? No, "without freshening it, the vitiated air, sending back upon them. . . ." The "vitiated air" is "sending back upon them?" No, the fan, it has to be. And note the "stale pomade," "stale breath," as if staleness is part of the natural "aftermath of sixty-two rainless days," a huge and pus-filled listlessness in the townsfolk that makes their nerves smolder for a violation of their bitterest prejudice, the hint of mixed blood or, worse, interracial rape. Well . . . no one knows exactly what's happened, but by story's end it's clearly Miss Minnie, not the men in the barber shop, who's been attacked, insulted, frightened—or so she thinks. Nobody knows for sure.

Readers caught up in Faulkner's cadences float on an emotional logic that overrides sense as they drift toward some far-off period. "Dry September" and *The Color Purple* both grab our shirts from their first words and we fall like a sweatdrop onto the page. We get hints of rape and the facts on incest and expect graphic sexual excitement. But both Faulkner and Walker repay us much more richly than their openings suggest. In all his stories and novels, Faulkner, as most white writers must, watches his Negroes from a distance, however sympathetic he is toward and admiring of their "enduring." This is his deepest word for them, one he uses in his early novel *The Sound and the Fury* (1929), then repeats about mankind generally in his Nobel Prize speech (1950). For me, he has only one fully rounded Negro, Lucas Beauchamp of *Intruder in the Dust* (1948), who carries the same weight on the page as Alice Walker's Negroes from the twenties and thirties. She, of course, enters her blacks with a centeredness Faulkner never attempts, and gives them a power of "enduring" he could match only in abstractions about them. In fact, the curse of abstraction makes his beloved Dilsey of *The Sound and the Fury* fall apart in the later pages, and the Negro in "Dry September" is merely a type, the victim of an ageing hysterical white spinster who thinks she's been raped. How or why she thinks this, we're never told, although the town thinks she's been taken in "adultery" (fornication, really) with a long gone middle-aged widower who had a whisky flush and seemingly led her into becoming a steady tippler. Nor do we ever know *how* the Negro is murdered, since Faulkner's storytelling lust dismisses such grisliness as mere newsprint.

The story's triple triumph lies in capturing the overblown blusterers who seek a victim for their soul-deep discomfort with themselves, and in giving us a brilliant fix on sexual hysteria and the spinster's psychic being, as when she goes to the movies after the murder:

> . . . Her lips began to tingle. . . . The lights flicked away; the screen glowed silver, and soon life began to unfold, beautiful and passionate and sad, while still the young men and girls entered, scented and sibilant in the half dark, their paired backs in silhouette delicate and sleek, their slim, quick bodies awkward, divinely young, while beyond them the silver dream accumulated, inevitably on and on.

The third triumph lies in Faulkner's infectious power of description:

> The barber went swiftly up the street where the spare lights, insect-swirled, glared in rigid and violent suspension in the lifeless air. The day had died in a pall of dust; above the darkened square, shrouded by the spent dust, the sky was as clear as the inside of a brass bell. Below the east was a rumor of the twice-waxed moon.

I don't know what largeness a "twice-waxed" moon bears (this September has had two full moons?), but the redness of the word "rumor" and the opening sentence's "bloody September twilight" lets my mind work in its richest inks. But, in fact, has the moon even risen? How do we know it's twice-waxed if it's only a rumor? Well, again, no reader knows exactly what's happened—and that's the art of it.

> None of them knew the color of the sky. Their eyes glanced level, and were fastened upon the waves that swept toward them. These waves were of the hue of slate, save for the tops, which were of foaming white, and all of the men knew the colors of the sea. The horizon narrowed and widened, and dipped and rose, and at all times its edge was jagged with waves that seemed thrust up in points like rocks.
> —"The Open Boat" (1898), *Maggie and Other Short Stories*, Stephen Crane

Wow.

Again we find Twain's stripped line at work, not a breath of rhetoric nor a fancy syllable in sight. Detail follows detail, and yet, the sentence rhythms lift each word above mere record of fact and pitch the lines at great eloquence. The striking forcefulness comes in part from the hardness of the images, things are slate and jagged and have points thrust up like rocks. You could scratch a match on this paragraph.

What about "None of them knew the color of the sky"? It's a color left out, the sea itself is so incredibly dangerous. We don't know just how dangerous at first, but surely we are hit by the disorienting fact that no one knows the color of the sky. Outdoors, why wouldn't we know that? Well, because our lives are slipping up and down these slate troughs. I get upset just thinking about it.

It takes longer to savor "all of the men knew the colors of the sea." On first reading this hit me as a dip in immediacy. Of course sailors know the colors of the sea, so what. What's new here is that we are placed *on* the sea and staring down into a shark's teeth, or at shark's teeth in the foaming white points of rock gliding toward us. We are spellbound by the color of death lapping about us.

The fourteenth child of a Methodist minister in New Jersey, Crane died at twenty-nine, in 1900, in Paris, having seven years earlier published his masterpiece *The Red Badge of Courage*. To me, by the way, the red badge is a bloody battle wound, but I think Crane means it to be more of a *thing* than a metaphor, a real badge you might buy in a five-and-dime or pawn shop, something you could hold in your palm, but now is pinned to a soldier's blouse. Like *The Color Purple, The Red Badge of Courage* is a novel written about the era just before the writer's birth, and like *The Color Purple*, it is largely hearsay from survivors, in Crane's case, of the Civil War, raised into hard, touchable fact, with each bit of book research given a lyric underpinning. "The Open Boat," an even flintier work than the unflinching *The Red Badge of Courage*, seeks a strippedness meant to show the flat indifference of nature to its creatures—and also to dazzle fellow writers who use too many words. Of course, it helps that he was actually aboard a ship that sank, and then spent thirty hours rowing a ten-foot dinghy. This jaw-chattering exposure, tied in with tuberculosis, helped kill him three years later. So, if a poet like Crane can't tell us the color of the sky, his eyes must be elsewhere, with the boat only six inches above water and a fat shark slashing about.

Let's add that there's a nice bunch of Twain's black humors afloat in this boat:

> A singular disadvantage of the sea lies in the fact that after successfully surmounting one wave, you discover that there is another behind it just as important and just as nervously anxious to do something effective in the way of swamping boats. In a ten-foot dinghy one can get an idea of the resources of the sea in the line of waves that is not

probable to the average experience which is never at sea in a dinghy.

And:

> The little boat, lifted by each towering sea and splashed viciously by the crests . . . seemed just a wee thing wallowing, miraculously top up, at the mercy of five oceans. Occasionally a great spread of water, like white flames, swarmed into her.
> "Bail her, Cook," said the captain serenely.
> "All right, Captain," said the cheerful cook.

I think Twain would have read "at the mercy of five oceans" with delight and envy, then marveled as we all do at the "water, like white flames, swarmed into her." *Ooooh-umh!*

Okay, Crane can write, can handle action and danger like a poet. But what about *this* Promethean stuff:

> Some of the evil of my tale may have been inherent in our circumstances. For years we lived anyhow with one another in the naked desert, under the indifferent heaven. By day the hot sun fermented us; and we were dizzied by the beating wind. At night we were stained by dew, and shamed into pettiness by the innumerable silences of stars. We were a self-centered army without parade or gesture, devoted to freedom, the second of man's creeds, a purpose so ravenous that it devoured all our strength, a hope so transcendent that our earlier ambitions faded in its glare.
> As time went by our need to fight for the ideal increased to an unquestioning possession, riding with spur and rein over our doubts. Willy, nilly it became a faith. We had sold ourselves into its slavery, manacled ourselves together in its chain-gang, bowed ourselves to serve its holiness with all

our good and ill content. The mentality of ordinary human slaves is terrible—they have lost the world—and we had surrendered, not body alone, but soul to the overmastering greed of victory. By our own act we were drained of morality, of volition, of responsibility, like dead leaves in the wind.

The everlasting battle stripped from us care of our own lives or of others'. We had ropes about our necks, and on our heads prices which showed that the enemy intended hideous tortures for us if we were caught. Each day some of us passed; and the living knew themselves just sentient puppets on God's stage: indeed, our taskmaster was merciless, merciless, so long as our bruised feet could stagger forward on the road. The weak envied those tired enough to die; for success looked so remote, and failure a near and certain, if sharp, release from toil. We lived always in the stretch or sag of nerves, either on the crest or in the troughs of waves of feeling. This impotency was bitter to us, and made us live only for the seen horizon, reckless what spite we inflicted or endured, since physical sensation showed itself meanly transient. Gusts of cruelty, perversions, lusts ran lightly over the surface without troubling us; for the moral laws which had seemed to hedge about these silly accidents must be yet fainter words. We had learned that there were pangs too sharp, griefs too deep, ecstasies too high for our finite selves to register. When emotion reached this pitch the mind choked; and memory went white till the circumstances were humdrum once more.

—*The Seven Pillars of Wisdom* (1926), T. E. Lawrence

Homeric language! Lawrence calls down the Muse, asks for a tongue of flame. I pitch this book on Olympus, he tells us, and promises thunderbolts. What force! Thrilling stuff, and what's more he delivers. Does *Seven Pillars* bog down here and there? It does. But here is a massive reading experience, told with as much truth as Lawrence could muster.

Did you like that opening? Look how it circles around on itself:

> Some of the evil of my tale may have been inherent in our circumstances. For years we lived anyhow with one another in the naked desert, under the indifferent heaven. . . . When emotion reached this pitch the mind choked; and memory went white till the circumstances were humdrum once more.

We go from circumstances under the indifferent heaven through full symphonic release back to circumstances humdrum once more. Ah, memory goes white in the naked strangeness and pain.

But what is he telling us? That this is a tale of evil. And that some of the evil sprang from circumstances. And the sun fermented us, we were dizzied, stained, shamed, we were self-centered, devoted, full of a purpose so ravenous that it devoured all our strength, a hope so transcendent that our earlier ambitions faded in its glare. So perhaps you will forgive any lapses with my teacup.

I think he's begging our indulgence, or he wouldn't have mentioned the upcoming evil, and fobbed it off as desert delirium. Those earlier ambitions that faded in the transcendent glare of hope, they were pure-hearted, not evil? Whose ambitions are they, Lawrence's personal ambitions, Arab ambitions, British ambitions, mankind's ambitions—we must wait and see. Anyway, for promised pangs too sharp, griefs too deep, ecstasies too high for our finite selves to register, we can be patient.

And enough nit-picking. I surrender. Now where have we heard such unusual phrases before, such as the ravenous devouring of our strength; bowed ourselves to serve its holiness with all our good and ill content; greed of victory; drained of morality like dead leaves in the wind; the everlasting battle; release from toil; in the stretch or sag of nerves; on the crest or in the trough of waves; and the wonderful "reckless what spite we inflicted or endured, since physical sensation showed itself meanly transient. Gusts of cruelty, perversions, lusts ran lightly over the surface without troubling us; for the moral laws which had seemed to hedge about these silly accidents must be yet fainter words."

Don't you get a Biblical feeling about all this? The *King James* translators have this same high eloquence and richness of moral metaphor. Need we whisper Sir Thomas Browne once more, and his picture of urn burial by Romans of their bones and ashes:

> Now since these dead bones have already out-lasted the living ones of Methuselah, and in a yard under ground, and thin walls of clay, outworn all the strong and specious buildings above it; and quietly rested under the drums and tramplings of three conquests; What Prince can promise such diuturnity unto his Reliques, or might not gladly say, *Sic ego componi versus in ossa velim.*
>
> Time which antiquates Antiquities, and hath an art to make dust of all things, hath yet spared these minor Monuments. . . . If we begin to die when we live, and long life be but a prolongation of death; our life is a sad composition; We live with death, and die not in a moment. How many pulses made up the life of Methuselah, were work for Archimedes.

"Hydrotaphia, or Urn-Burial" was published in 1658, or 48 years after the *King James Bible*, of whose mind-stretching metaphors Sir Thomas clearly had drunk deep. And so had another of Browne's followers, Sir Charles Doughty, whose *Travels in Arabia Deserta* Lawrence revered. Doughty's clotted Biblical cadences go too far, but Lawrence loved the old man anyway and attended his funeral. I won't quote him, since I've made my point that Lawrence's great originality was not a date palm sprung full-blown from the sand. In fact, he wrote the first paragraphs in 1919, then lost his manuscript, and a month later began "to scribble out what I could remember. . . . Naturally the style was careless" and he thought the whole work "hopelessly bad" and in 1922 burned his corrected text of *Seven Pillars*. Only a hero like the writer of our first paragraphs above would burn a corrected second draft. Burning a first draft, sure, we get carried away. But a corrected second draft (after having lost the entire first draft), *burned*? That's painful.

Seven Pillars of Wisdom went through numberless rewritings, was edited for Lawrence by George Bernard Shaw (and his wife, Charlotte), and published in 1926, when Lawrence was thirty-eight. He lived only nine more years (having enlisted as a private in the Tank Corps and then the Air Force) and came to regret his Promethean style in *Seven Pillars*, spoke of it slightingly among his enlisted mates and in his letters. He would admit, however, that his book was "all spiritually true" about his early days as a man of action. He had dreamed that *Seven Pillars* would be a titanic English work on the scale of "*The Karamazovs, Zarathustra* and *Moby Dick*." But he wrote to Thomas Hardy's wife, Florence: "It was meant to be the true history of a political movement whose essence was a fraud, in the sense that its leaders did not believe the arguments with which they moved its rank and file. . . ." And yet, those dizzying first paragraphs, the white glare of transcendent hope! Where did the fraud end? In *King James*, one believes the metaphors, they ring to the bottom of our being. How far can we trust Lawrence's marvels of language?

Why not just accept *Seven Pillars of Wisdom* wholeheartedly as a work of art rather than history.

Lawrence's opening asks the Muse for a charge to carry him through his historical poem; it crackles at the beginning like a Red Devil car battery for him to lay his hand on should energy waver; for his will be a huge spending of genius. What if he had begun more modestly but with the same scope as Tolstoy's opening:

The Assyrian King, Esarhaddon, had conquered the kingdom of King Lailie, had destroyed and burnt the towns, taken all the inhabitants captive to his own country, slaughtered the warriors, beheaded some chieftans and impaled or flayed others, and had confined King Lailie himself in a cage.

Such modesty was always possible. But it would not have been Lawrence's voice, or, let's say, Lawrence's writing voice in those years of his life. We know that Lawrence was extremely modest, shy, and unself-serving while well aware of his own fantastic mind and language skills. But on the desert he had killed men with his own hands, personally executed others, been subjected to torture and homosexual rape. He had mixed with the wiliest, least stable, rigid Arab mentalities who held great power over their peoples, and under the desert sun he had been baked to the leathery hardness of the damned. With that background, polite history did not fit the spirit of the events. He needed a great wind from above to fill out his voice and sound his story true. So what is the nature of that wind? Robert Graves suggests an answer:

Since the age of fifteen poetry has been my ruling passion and I have never intentionally undertaken any task or formed any relationship that seemed inconsistent with poetic principles; which has sometimes won me the reputation of an eccentric. Prose has been my livelihood, but I have used it as a means of sharpening my sense of the altogether different nature of poetry, and the themes that I choose are always linked in my mind with outstanding poetic problems. At the age of sixty-five I am still amused at the paradox of poetry's obstinate continuance in the present phase of civilization. Though recognized as a learned profession it is the only one for the study of which no academies are open and in which there is no yard-stick, however crude, by which technical proficiency is considered measurable. 'Poets are born, not made.' The deduction that one is expected to draw from this is that the nature of poetry is too mysterious to bear examination: is, indeed, a greater mystery even than royalty, since kings can be made as well as born and the quoted utterances of a dead king carry little weight either in the pulpit or the public bar.

—*The White Goddess* (1948), Robert Graves

Now this is both personal and Olympian. Graves at the start of a vast, outrageous, intensely romantic, rhapsodical bodying forth of a magical being at the core of his poetic powers, disarms us with a voice pitched firm and low, and speaking companionably to the reader. He has no need to call on the Muse in his first paragraph, since his whole book will be about her ("a greater mystery than royalty"), and she will carry us to places that stagger our sense of what writing's all about. And he's telling himself not to give the show away too quickly.

Graves's standing as a poet was not great when—at sixty-five—he published *The White Goddess*; he was more esteemed as a novelist, especially of the bestsellers *I, Claudius* and *Claudius the God*, while his autobiography, *Goodbye to All That*, was acclaimed the greatest memoir of trench life in World War One. What's more, Graves himself revised his large body of verse time and again to make its song an homage to his Muse, The White Goddess, and for decades this kept his collected poems in an ever-slippery, oily mass of changed lines, dropped stanzas, lopped off poems. *The White Goddess* at last plugged the reader's finger into a wall socket and lighted up the guest in Graves's house.

Graves, one of those terrible people who always say what they think, was as opinionated as a swordblade—sometimes a bent swordblade. This in part was a defense against the long-lingering effects of shellshock, which left him a rambling, unfocused, insecure man with opinions of steel. Then he met one of those unsettling, X-ray intelligences, a poetess, who was a Russian Jew, who skewered him top to bottom and put the pieces back together as Robert Graves, Poet. O, Isis and Osiris, a familiar story! He left his wife and four children to live in happy agony with Laura Riding, the poetess, for many years, until they parted. I will not characterize Laura, except to say that from her photographs she was not beautiful and, in fact, looked like a small-chinned, large-nosed Hittite princess and night and day wore a tiara that spelled LAURA. Graves saw more in her than this. She was his post in a shell-shocked world. Soon all of his poetry circled about her while all the housework and cooking—which he did willingly—circled about him. But life with LAURA and fear of losing it led him into such psychic torment that, several years after they'd parted, he became crazed with the need to thumb together a figure of the moon goddess, his Muse, and wrote *The White Goddess*.

Graves's goddess becomes more than Laura Riding. His book, he said later, "is about how a poet thinks." It's a myth that puts together many earlier myths, overrides them and, in the figure of the goddess, becomes the poet's moon, his lunacy, his mother and lover, and bodywasher when dead. Without footnotes or named sources, Graves builds a grammar of myths springing from Neolithic times, when woman was worshipped, before Greek logicians supplanted the breath-giving goddess myth with mere philosophy, and before the Hebrews wheeled Abraham, Isaac and Jacob onstage.

The character of the goddess terrifies. She shakes the poet's earth, demands absolute adoration. Less than that, and he's a mere greeting-card wordsmith. She wants his blood. This is no idle crush on Calliope, the Muse of epic poetry, or on Euterpe, the Muse of lyric poetry. She wants his last penny. She wants *everything*. The tension that makes the poems knot up and start singing on the line is the tough-mindedness of the poet, his manliness, his unsentimental, hard pull back against her while willing into the goddess even more energy from his stores. He must die in her service, and be replaced.

All things that glow from his head feed her heart. She lives on, followed by whorls

> in Time made
> By the strong pulling of her bladed mind
> —from "On Portents"

That's not such a bad thought for a Western writer, who might otherwise be swearing by Judeo-Christian folk wisdom, the Voice that threads the Bible and blows words into waving wheat. One wonders what the goddess thinks of the songs of David. Or one could be reaching down for the dark blood-consciousness of D. H. Lawrence, not a bad place to drink. But, perhaps in the end, the choice is between creating one's own moon myth or being sucked into a pre-existing myth, for Graves's White Goddess is made of his own being, while David adores the Lord who covers Himself with light as with a robe, stretches out the heavens like a starry curtain, lays the beams of His house in the waters, and demands to be admired as intensely as the goddess demands of Graves. David, his head shining with oil in firelight, strings his harp, Graves plants his staff on the moon and both await a divinity to give them song.

But what of Graves's prose, without the goddess? Why does he choose the particular voice he chooses above? I've accounted for what he says, his restraint. But what about his *sound*? Here is the third paragraph from his handbook for writers of English prose:

> English is a vernacular of vernaculars. It began in the
> eleventh century as the lingo used between the Norman-
> French conquerors and their Anglo-Saxon serfs, and though
> it became a literary language in the fourteenth century has
> never crystallized in the way that Italian, French and
> Spanish have done. A proof of this is that no writer of
> English would be credited with a perfect literary style merely
> because he had exactly modelled himself on some native

paragon—say, Addison in England, or Emerson in the United States—as Italians, Spaniards and Frenchmen might be after modelling themselves, respectively, on Boccaccio, Cervantes and Bossuet. To write English well, it is generally agreed, is not to imitate, but to evolve a style peculiarly suited to one's own temperament, environment and purposes. English has never been jealously watched over by a learned Academy, as French has been since the seventeenth century; nor protected against innovations either by literary professionalism, as with Italian, or, as with Spanish, by the natural decorum of the greater part of those who use it. It is, indeed, an immense, formless aggregate not merely of foreign assimilations and local dialects but of occupational and household dialects and personal eccentricities.

> —*The Reader Over Your Shoulder* (1943),
> Robert Graves and Alan Hodge

Now that pins down a tangled matter so clearly that you can take it in on one reading—and without holding your breath for syntax to work itself out. This great handbook lights up dark bogs in your paragraph, those swamped sentences where the brain fades and only a crane can lift you out. It's not about poetry, just clear thought, which is my point. In *The White Goddess* Graves knows that he sails into twice-dark seas, beyond the edge of history and the reach of literature. He is about to invent his psyche. You don't mention stuff like that in the first paragraph. The first page of *The White Goddess* delays adopting the poet/scholar's or poet/historian's vernacular Graves will use throughout and is instead high-toned chit-chat so clear that—without thought—the reader turns the page and is into the book. This sweetens us with thoughts like, Nothing fearful here, and Gosh, I'm a bit like Graves myself! You aren't, and he doesn't say that, but you tie that love knot anyway.

It was nearly sunset. High above the broad valley gigantic shafts of mellowing sunlight slanted down majestically to the earth. Far away, miles away, endless green fields of spring wheat swelled heavily, emulating the motions of the sea. A coldish wind, which had arisen deep in central Africa and cooled on its flight to the Mediterranean, swooped off the mountain tops still glistening vaguely where the snow had not melted. The pilots, most of them, said little as they walked along the flight line out to the place where the photographer had set up his tripod. Taking the official squadron portrait the day before they were going up to meet the Luftwaffe for the first time made them edgy. Those who were proud or elated kept it to themselves and hoped to get copies of the picture soon.

Nervously, bumping each other awkwardly in a rush of subdued excitement, they lined up four abreast, by flights. On the grass off to one side, the ground crewmen, in soiled khaki fatigues, lounged around the chuckwagon, eating their lunch of pea soup, boiled eggs, and sandwiches. They found the pilots an interesting group: glory-seeking, headstrong, quick to take up unusual challenges, smart-talking, and a little oblivious to things, a little too anxious to hold their heads higher than a black was supposed to.
—*The Homestead Grays* (1977), James Wylie

What's right about this opening? It starts with a majestic image of gigantic sunslants in an evening valley. We see far-off wheatfields moving, are chilled with a cold wind, take in snowtopped summer mountains somewhere near the Mediterranean (or perhaps Africa), are told a picture is about to be taken of some fresh pilots who are going up against the Luftwaffe for the first time. Ah, air war! Our interest is caught but hangs fire. Something more must come.

As pilots form with mild excitement four abreast, we watch them being watched by ground crewmen eating pea soup, boiled eggs, and sandwiches. The crewmen find the pilots interesting types. Why? At last we are told. Fresh for battle, this is a black squadron, full of beans, more than a bit uppity.

Wylie takes this scene, with quiet irony since it's about black pilots, not white, from the first paragraph of a William Faulkner short story about World War One pilots (Wylie reprints the Faulkner paragraph as one of his epigraphs):

> In pictures, the snapshots hurriedly made, a little faded, a little dog-eared with the thirteen years, they swagger a little. Lean, hard, in their brass-and-leather harness, posed standing beside or leaning upon the esoteric shapes of wire and wood and canvas in which they flew without parachutes, they too have an esoteric look; a look not exactly human, like that of some dim and threatful apotheosis of the race seen for an instant in the glare of a thunderclap and then forever gone.
> —"All the Dead Pilots" (1931), *Collected Stories*, William Faulkner

So what are the differences here? Well, Faulkner is writing a short story and makes every word carry both meaning and a charge of eloquence. First he appeals to our nostalgia for faded pictures, then draws us out of ourselves by an appeal to our sense of the esoteric, that these planes are the secret machines of wizards, then to our sense of danger since these air devils flew without parachutes, then he shows us the men themselves, "not exactly human," and then lets go his big gun, raising his pilots to godhood—but a brief godhood, "seen for an instant in the glare of a thunderclap and then forever gone."

Not everybody writes this well. Wylie has a long novel ahead of him and keeps the reader relaxed, avoids Faulkner's daring sentence structure (Faulkner has only two sentences), gives us some scenery, then lets the facts march forward and work on our sense of danger, humor and surprise. This is, in fact, a style Wylie puts behind him in later novels, where he strives for much more poetry in every area of his tales. By the bye, I'd take out the *the* in "A coldish wind . . . swooped off the mountain tops still glistening vaguely where the snow had not melted"; *the* stops us to think about whether the wind or the mountain tops still glisten(s) vaguely.

Lest you think I put Wylie unfairly up against Faulkner, here's my starred Kirkus review of *The Homestead Grays*, which appeared two months before the novel's pub date in 1977. Reviews in *Kirkus Reviews* alert libraries, movie agents, the publishing world and so on to forthcoming titles, and a starred review stands out strongly:

> A brainy, flame-grained, profoundly felt air-combat novel about the only all-black fighter squadron in WW II. The Homestead Grays are named after a black baseball team in the South, and their squadron offers the first opportunity for blacks to achieve a tremendous symbolic victory using sophisticated machinery (Mustangs) while fighting for a country that keeps them on the ground and underfoot. These heroes are blacks of the 1930s, half-blind with depression, whose lives are suddenly lighted by the thunderclap of a war that draws their blood up into high flame—before burning them to white ash. The story follows them through North Africa, Sicily, and France in a thorough depiction of every aspect of air war, plus the logistics of ground battle. Wylie wrings maximum altitude out of his Mustang pilots and the horrors of the cockpit. And, at novel's end, the prop-driven black aces engage the first German jet squadron in a contest over Berlin that shakes with doom. Fact-as-exhilarating myth, this delivers full force, exploding and fading with a direct hit on the adrenals and sympathetic ganglia.

In the trade, that's called a selling review. But the novel sold very little, though it later saw an Avon mass-market edition before being pulped. Nor did it receive the three major reviews needed to make the *Book Review Digest*, a useful annual found in most libraries as a guide to book reviews. This novel went down unsung, even though Wylie writes wonderfully about air battles (that may be where the flame-grained prose is), has a strong feel for blacks in the Army Air Corps, for the funk of black life in Washington, D.C. during the war, and gives a climax that is sheer Gotterdammerung, the twilight of the black aces over Berlin when they come up against Messerschmitt jets and are ripped to shreds. Ah, the sadness!

Reading *The Homestead Grays* I thought Wylie a white man with an enviable skill for seeing into blacks. I later found that it was a skill he was born with, being black; and that there were four all-black American air squadrons in World War II.

And here's another pilot, this time a woman:

> How is it possible to bring order out of memory? I should like to begin at the beginning, patiently, like a weaver at his loom. I should like to say, "This is the place to start; there can be no other."
>
> But there are a hundred places to start for there are a hundred names—Mwanza, Serengetti, Nungwe, Molo, Nakuru. There are easily a hundred names, and I can begin best by choosing one of them—not because it is first nor of any importance in a wildly adventurous sense, but because here it happens to be, turned uppermost in my logbook. After all, I am no weaver. Weavers create. This is remembrance—revisitation; and names are keys that open corridors no longer fresh in the mind, but nonetheless familiar in the heart.
>
> —*West with the Night* (1942), Beryl Markham

Two styles rule writing in English, the stripped and the ornamental. Sometimes the ornamental style devours the writer's voice, and often the stripped, a brief record of fact and sensation, is drained of voice. This very paragraph has no voice. Beryl Markham's voice weaves in and out of her style, sometimes speaks right to us, or turns lyric, feelingful and well-written—but is not quite a living voice.

Style is the tie of the writer to the reader. How may I serve you best in telling you my story? Should I wrap you in words—or grab your shirt? And what will serve my story best? Some years ago (more than thirty), Norman Mailer came upon *nuance*, and style for him became nuance, a suggestiveness that thrived on the underside of things, the unsaid or unsayable, and his line turned into a metaphor-rich scraggle as the reader doubled up in knots trying to grasp Mailer's nuances and unveilings of psychic layers. This was the high of the sixties, and Mailer wrote for cats and hipsters, Zen folk and potheads. But ten years later, set forth upon the huge sea of *The Executioner's Song*, he vanished behind a faceless flow of de-metaphored information—for this was epic journalism and any nuance must be made plain. The style had gone public and was meant for readers who bought *Life* and had memberships in the Book-of-the-Month Club. He won the Pulitzer Prize for this searing but un-Mailerlike work.

West with the Night went out of print, then leaped to vast bestsellerdom fifty years later, largely because Markham cuts an exciting figure as a literary stylist, a racehorse breeder, a pilot flying the mail and saving lives in the African night and being the first woman pilot to cross the Atlantic east-to-west in solo flight. In her first paragraph she adds her frou-frou about the weaver to an otherwise smart opening. Drop "patiently, like a weaver at his loom," and the paragraph sings. The next paragraph moves smartly until that poetical weaver turns up again, in a sentence no one believes: "After all, I am no weaver." But that's just what she is, a wordweaver, for whom truth is not always uppermost. What are we to make of this:

> It is absurd for a man to kill an elephant. It is not brutal, it is not heroic, and certainly it is not easy; it is just one of

those preposterous things that men do like putting a dam
across a great river, one tenth of whose volume could engulf
the whole of mankind without disturbing the domestic life
of a single catfish. (p. 205)

This is posturing. Whom for? Fellow women? Are women
expected to accept that killing an elephant is like damming a
river? What does "one tenth of whose volume could engulf the
whole of mankind" mean? That she sees the neat possibility of
drowning everyone on earth, man and woman, in one-tenth
of the water of this shadowy dam? Is this a dam on the Congo?
On Lake Victoria? Does she hate Hoover Dam? Are there
catfish in Kenya? What happens is that she asks the reader to
slide over her weak likening of a death and dam by the force
of her prejudices, just as she wants us to accept her pose as a
weaver and poet. Drop "After all, I am no weaver. Weavers
create," and her second paragraph is at once stronger. Not
perfect, but stronger. "Wildly adventurous" looks forward, not
artfully, and feels forced—another Yes wrapped up in a No,
"I'm not wildly adventurous"—a defense against a thought
the reader never had. Just as she tells us, "But I am no knight.
I am no knight that would earn the greeting of any other save
perhaps of that fabulous and pathetic one who quested the by-
paths of a distant and more ancient Spain" (p. 137). Is she or
isn't she a knight? Does this ass-rubbing with Don Quixote
offend me? I think she paints herself, not him, as fabulous and
nobly pathetic, Beryl the unstained. So which sentiments
anywhere in this memoir are truthful?

Don't think I don't admire *West with the Night*. Here's a
passage where her grand manner pays off. She and her lover,
big game hunter Bror Blixen, have just flown to Benghazi and
their Arab taxi driver can't find them a hotel room except in
"a web-work of pinched and broken streets, dark, swept with
the odours of poverty, the trapped and stagnant smells of
stagnant life":

A door opened down the yard and a woman came toward us. She had a lighted candle and she lifted it close to our faces. Her own face held the lineage of several races, none of which had given it distinction. It was just a husk with eyes. She spoke, but we understood nothing. Hers was a language neither of us had ever heard.

Blix made gestures with his hands, asking for rooms, and the woman nodded quickly enough and led us into the house and up a flight of stairs. She showed us two rooms not even separated by a door. Each contained an iron bed that cowered under a sticky blanket and had an uncovered pillow at its head. One room had a white enamel basin on the floor, and the jug to match it was on the floor of the other. Everything lay under scales of filth.

"All the diseases of the world live here," I said to Blix.

He was laconic. "So do we, until tomorrow." (p. 267)

Here's a first paragraph by a friend of Markham's whose book appeared five years earlier than hers:

I had a farm in Africa, at the foot of the Ngong Hills. The Equator runs across these highlands, a hundred miles to the North, and the farm lay at an altitude of over six thousand feet. In the day-time you felt that you had got high up, near to the sun, but the early mornings and evenings were limpid and restful, and the nights were cold.
—*Out of Africa* (1937), Isak Dinesen

Before writing *Out of Africa*, Isak Dinesen, or Karen Blixen, had already published *Seven Gothic Tales* (1934), a witch's amusements boiling in a smooth upflow and bubbling of imagination in the alpha state. She trusted her unconscious to lead her through a bizarre luxuriance into the dream-flowering of the story's shape and darker meanings, down a glowy path tinted by a Scandinavian sense of fate cupped over the reader as night falls. When she came to write *Out of Africa*, none of this Scandinavian twilight would be right for her purposes and she turned to Mnemosyne, the Muse of memory, and mother of all Nine Muses, and drew art and breath from clear African light six thousand feet up. As she tells us in her second paragraph:

> . . . the height of the land combined to create a landscape
> that had not its like in all the world. There was no fat on it
> and no luxuriance anywhere; it was Africa distilled up
> through six thousand feet, like the strong and refined
> essence of a continent. The colors were dry and burnt, like
> the colors in pottery. The trees had a light delicate foliage,
> the structure of which was different from that of the trees in
> Europe. . . .

Beryl Markham asks us, "How is it possible to bring order out of memory?" Yet she does not trust Mnemosyne all the way, falling back on catalogues of fact any journalist could drum up, and inventing a sentimental alter ego with which to bolster her page. Isak Dinesen draws memory from a deeper well and seeks the heart of Africa, the essence, not its skin. So, the two writers differ as a talent and a genius. Markham will fly hither and about, putting her record together, with flash and show. Isak Dinesen sits still and drops like a stone into memory. And this is the difference in character between the two women: Dinesen is centered while Markham works like a magpie, picking up every stray rag. But this is one of the qualities I happen to like about Markham, that in her later revisions she reshuffles her scenes and chapters so that—not strict with time—they imitate memory at full surge. Form energizes her and is a briefcase into which she can stuff any incident. That appeals to the beginner. But Isak Dinesen has already learned the payoff that comes with being in charge of her material. She *does* make order out of memory. She trusts her Muse.

How does Dinesen's first paragraph work? Rather like God saying Let there be light, she says Let there be Africa, but an Africa of the past, with a farm in Eden one hundred miles below the Equator, and high up, near the sun, with the light at six thousand feet limpid and restful, and the nights cold. She just says it.

Is there some special rhythm or cadence, choice of words, heightening or pitch of language? Not for me. And yet I know this is Isak Dinesen just as I know my wife's hand running through my hair in bed is my wife's. It must be some intimacy, some current from her. For many years I was tone-deaf about writing and could not grasp the notion of a voice in fiction, or nonfiction. I could hear stories in dialect, of course. But that language itself had a voice was something I didn't hear, at heart wouldn't believe, and thought was a phony idea. The voice of our most famed essayist, E. B. White, escaped me for thirty years; I heard nothing, whenever I read him, and saw fancy, rather thin writing. Today I hear and admire it. Again, I could tell the styles of various literary periods, from the sentence construction, the general clottedness of writing in earlier centuries. I *saw* the Hemingway sentence, loped along with the Faulknerian cadence, swam with Thomas Wolfe—but as for voice . . . all a mystery. Perhaps I had to listen to thousands of pages of my own breathing to begin to hear others. My ear canals began picking up echoes from poets. The poetry I wrote was as tone-deaf as the next man's, and still is—it takes an unbelievably precious gift for a poet to speak directly to his reader. Without that gift you will imitate a thousand things and always be a leaden knockoff of the real thing. The voice in writing arises from the way the writer speaks to the reader, a kind of moral intimacy or measuring of honesty in what's being said.

> One dark night,
> my Tudor Ford climbed the hill's skull;
> I watched for love-cars. Lights turned down,

they lay together, hull to hull,
where the graveyard shelves the town. . . .
My mind's not right.

A car radio bleats,
"Love, O careless Love . . ." I hear
my ill-spirit sob in each blood cell,
as if my hand were at its throat . . .
I myself am hell;
nobody's here—
   —from "Skunk Hour," *Life Studies* (1964),
                                    Robert Lowell

Lowell writing about himself speaks right at you, almost with a glare, his one-on-one holds you spellbound, and the voice is unmistakably his. (You don't ask how his hand can be at the throat of an ill-spirit sob in a blood cell—you just accept the force of it.) I measure honesty. Hear it. Is the writer faking, befuddled, posing, or really himself, not masked with borrowings from the literary wardrobe. When Dinesen lifts me into the limpid, restful light six thousand feet above the plains and then adds the night chill, I feel safe, and I find that the slightly homesick voice telling me of her East African hill farm engages me by the distance at which she keeps her pain as she unfolds her tale. "I had a farm in Africa, at the foot of the Ngong hills. . . ."

   Nobody could sleep. When morning came, assault craft
   would be lowered and a first wave of troops would ride
   through the surf and charge ashore on the beach at
   Anopopei. All over the ship, all through the convoy, there
   was a knowledge that in a few hours some of them were
   going to be dead.
             —*The Naked and the Dead* (1948), Norman Mailer

At twenty-five here is Mailer the naturalist, a first-novelist keeping his sentence under tight rein, striving for mood, setting his hook under the reader's jaw. Looking back on this novel years later, he saw no originality in the journeyman style. This opening could have been written by a thousand American writers with no strain. Aside from vaulting ambition, the novel shows little of the Mailer who was to be the self-consciously irreverent and dangerous writer setting out "to change the consciousness of our time." It is memorable to me largely for its humor, its action, the novelty of the "Time Machine" device adapted from John Dos Passos, Mailer's drawing of the first intellectual I'd ever met in American fiction, General Cummings, and his modeling of the novel's climax on *Moby Dick*, and its last great chapters, "The Three-Day Chase," a big roll of the dice for such a young writer. He takes strength from Tolstoy in showing a large canvas of men at war, but the novel's compass is borrowed from Melville. At its birth in 1851, *Moby Dick* was a truly dangerous novel with a vision that blew Christian values to hell and gone, and Mailer now dared to echo Melville's depression and Godlessness with his own grey vision of white Anglo-Saxon Protestants at war. Mailer himself would later tell his biographer Peter Manso:

I didn't have much literary sophistication while writing *The Naked and the Dead*. I admired John Dos Passos immensely and wanted to write a book that would be like one of his. My novel was frankly derivative, directly derivative. A lot of the techniques, like the Time Machine, came out of Dos Passos, and while I was writing I kept saying to myself, "Gee, this isn't nearly as good as Dos Passos. I just don't have his gift."

I had four books on my desk all the time I was writing: *Anna Karenina, Of Time and the River, U.S.A.*, and *Studs Lonigan*. And whenever I wanted to get in the mood to write I'd read one of them. The atmosphere of *The Naked and the Dead*, the overspirit, is Tolstoyan; the rococo comes out of Dos Passos, the fundamental, slogging style from

Farrell, and the occasional overrich descriptions from Wolfe.

—*Mailer, His Life and Times* (1985), Peter Manso (p. 101)

Ten years later, *the* Norman Mailer had found his voice and even become dangerous with a style that had leaped from the stripped to baroque-ornamental, whose demands few living writers could match for richness and originality, although what he was saying was less compelling than how he was saying it. And how relaxed he sounds in this huge Proustian first paragraph! Remember also that he had taken a degree in engineering at Harvard, which may have helped his eye for the paragraph's materials and ear for sentence rhythms:

I was living in a room one hundred feet long and twenty-five feet wide, and it had nineteen windows staring at me from three of the walls and part of the fourth. The floor planks were worn below the level of the nails which held them down, except for the southern half of the room where I had laid a rough lineoleum which gave a hint of sprinkled sand, conceivably an aid to the footwork of my pupils. For one hundred dollars I had the place whitewashed; everything; the checkerboard of tin ceiling plates one foot square with their fleurs-de-lis stamped into the metal, the rotted sashes on the window frames (it took twelve hours to scrape the calcimine from the glass), even parts of the floor had white drippings (although that was scuffed into dust as time went on) and yet it was worth it: when I took the loft it stank of old machinery and the paint was a liverish brown—I had tried living with that color for a week, my old furniture, which had been moved by a mover friend from the Village and me, showed the scars of being bumped and dragged and flung up six flights of stairs, and the view of it sprawled over twenty-five hundred feet of living space, three beat old day beds, some dusty cushions, a broken-armed easy chair, a cigarette-scarred coffee table made from a door, a kitchen table, some peeled enamel chairs which thumped like a wooden-legged pirate when one sat in them, the bookshelves of unfinished pine butted by bricks, yes, all of this, my purview, this grand vista, the New York sunlight greeting me in the morning through the double filter of the smog-yellow sky and the nineteen dirt-frosted windows, inspired me with so much content, especially those liver-brown walls, that I fled my pad like the plague, and in the first week, after a day of setting the furniture to rights, I was there for four hours of sleep a night, from five in the morning when I maneuvered in from the last closed Village bar and the last coffee-klatsch of my philosopher friends' for the night to let us say nine in the morning when I awoke with a partially destroyed brain and the certainty that the sore vicious growl of my stomach was at least the onset of an ulcer and more likely the first gone cells of a thorough-going cancer of the duodenum. So I lived it that way for a week, and then following the advice of a bar-type who was the friend of a friend, I got myself up on the eighth morning, boiled my coffee on a hot-plate while I shivered in the October air (neither the stove nor the gas heaters had yet been bought) and then I went downstairs and out the front door of the warehouse onto Monroe Street, picking my way through the garbage-littered gutter which always made me think of the gangs on this street, the Negroes on the east end of the block, the Puerto Ricans next to them, and the Italians and Jews to the west—those gangs were going to figure a little in my life, I suspected that, I was anticipating those moments with no quiet bravery considering how hung was my head in the morning, for the worst clue to the gangs was the six-year-olds. They were the defilers of garbage, knights of the ordure, and here, in this province of a capital Manhattan, at the southern tip of the island, with the overhead girders of the Manhattan and

Brooklyn bridges the only noble structures for a mile of tenement jungle, yes here the barbarians ate their young, and any tyke who reached the age of six without being altogether mangled by father, mother, family or friends, was a pint of iron man, so tough, so ferocious, so sharp in the teeth that the wildest alley cat would have surrendered a freshly caught rat rather than contest the meal. They were charming, these six-year-olds, as I told my uptown friends, and they used to topple the overloaded garbage cans, strew them through the street, have summer snowball fights with orange peel, coffee grounds, soup bones, slop, they threw the discus by scaling the raw tin rounds from the tops of cans, their pillow fights were with loaded socks of scum, and a debauch was for two of them to scrub a third around the inside of a twenty-gallon pail still warm with the heat of its emptied treasures. I heard that the Olympics took place in summer when they were out of school and the streets were so thick with the gum of old detritus, alluvium and dross that the mash made by passing car tires fermented in the sun. Then the parents and the hoods and the debs and the grandmother dowagers cheered them on and promised them murder and the garbage flew all day, but I was there in fall and the scene was quiet from nine to three. So I picked my way through last night's stew of rubble on the eighth morning of my hiatus on Monroe Street, and went half down the block to a tenement on the boundary between those two bandit republics of the Negroes and the Puerto Ricans, and with a history or two of knocking on the wrong door, and with a nose full of the smells of the sick overpeppered bowels of the poor which seeped and oozed out of every leaking pipe in every communal crapper (only as one goes north does the world take on the Protestant propriety of john), I was able finally to find my man, and I was an hour ahead of him—he was still sleeping off his last night's drunk. So I spoke to his wife, a fat masculine

Negress with the face and charity of a Japanese wrestler,
and when she understood that I was neither a junk-peddler
nor fuzz, that I sold no numbers, carried no bills, and was
most certainly not a detective (though my Irish face left her
dubious of that) but instead had come to offer her husband
a job of work, I was admitted to the first of three dark
rooms, face to face with the gray luminescent eye of the
television set going its way in a dark room on a bright
morning, and through the hall curtains I could hear them
talking in the bedroom.

"Get up you son of a bitch," she said to him.

> —"The Time of Her Time" (1958), *Advertisements*
> *for Myself*, Norman Mailer

The voice is modest and confiding but the effect is of a tour
de force, with Mailer's new rippling biceps on show as he
flexes and unflexes huge, flowing sentences that never waver in
mastery of syntax while offering smelly nosegays of metaphor.
This is a python with a cobra's charm. Every syllable has its
just weight and space, no phrase gets crushed, no sentence
flaps away untrimmed. A lot of care went into this lacework,
the kind of happy descriptive genius behind Caliban's

> All the infections that the sun sucks up
> From bogs, fens, flats, on Prosper fall, and make him
> By inch-meal a disease! his spirits hear me
> . . . .
> For every trifle are they set upon me;
> Sometime like apes, that mow and chatter at me,
> And after bite me; then like hedgehogs, which
> Lie tumbling in my barefoot way, and mount
> Their pricks at my footfall; sometimes am I
> All wound with adders, who with cloven tongues
> Do hiss me into madness.

> —*The Tempest*, William Shakespeare (II, ii)

I don't believe in his report on the six year olds at the garbage Olympics and two rolling a third about in a hot garbage can, but I understand that he must center his catalogue of scums and stews and street mash on human figures—and, anyway, he says he didn't actually see it. If there is a flaw in this passage it's that the narrator, Sergius O'Shaugnessy, can't possibly write this well and is an idiot to do anything else if he can. What he does do in this huge studio loft is teach bullfighting, but this is Greenwich Village!

Now, quickly, we overleap many variations in the Mailer voice and arrive at *Ancient Evenings*, where the set pieces are even more refined and rich than the first paragraph of "The Time of Her Time," and the immense astral overview is anchored with shockingly intense physical detail. Again, as in *The Executioner's Song*, Mailer leaves aside his former public mask as literary clown-genius, and lets his characters do the talking. The opening two or three pages have a difficulty, in that the reader has no understanding, at first, that he is inside the soul of an Egyptian three thousand years ago who is now transmigrating through a surreal landscape to a new body:

Crude thoughts and fierce forces are my state. I do not know who I am. Nor what I was. I cannot hear a sound. Pain is near that will be like no pain felt before.

Is this the fear that holds the universe? Is pain the fundament? All the rivers veins of pain? The oceans my mind awash? I have a thirst like the heart of earth on fire. Mountains writhe. I see waves of flame. Washes, flashes, waves of flame.

Thirst is in the rivers of my body. The rivers burn but do not move. Flesh—is it flesh?—lies beneath some heated stone. Lava rises in burned-out fields.

Where, in what cavern, have such disruptions taken place? Volcanic lips give fire, wells bubble. Bone lies like rubble upon the wound.

Is one human? Or merely alive? Like a blade of grass

equal to all existence in the moment it is torn? Yes. If pain
is fundament, then a blade of grass can know all there is.
                    —*Ancient Evenings* (1983), Norman Mailer

A daring opening, with the prospect of readers dropping
away like flies. *Ancient Evenings* was savaged and trashed as a
seven-hundred-page blunder by *The New York Times Book
Review*'s reviewer, who then turned around a few months later
and gave a symphonic hero's welcome in those same pages to
Mark Helprin's *Winter's Tale*, a work I find to be artful marzi-
pan. Had Mailer written that book, a work well within his
powers, the reviewers' disgust with his selling out would have
been uncontainable, and if Helprin had published *Ancient
Evenings*, a work far beyond his powers, or anyone but Mailer's,
reviewers would have been stunned by Helprin's unbelievable
leap in inventive powers. But the world of criticism is imper-
fect and a list of great works battered on first publication would
start with *Moby Dick, Leaves of Grass, Les Fleurs du Mal, The
Adventures of Huckleberry Finn*, and *Anna Karenina*. As Mailer
said afterward, "Look, if a book is rich enough, it really
shouldn't be unanimously received." *Ancient Evenings* will out-
last its notices. For me, its characters are more fully rounded
and carry more psychological weight on the page than any
created by Faulkner, Hemingway, Fitzgerald or Wolfe, while
they exist in a fully rendered world of spirit undreamed of by
our celebrated Big Four.

Now leap another eight years, to 1991, with no new Nor-
mans inbetween, a writing silence taken up by the 1,334-page
Harlot's Ghost. Can there be a still newer Mailer voice? Richer,
deeper? Here are two first paragraphs from that novel,
one from the second chapter of Part One and one from a
later chapter (as I first read them in excerpt in *Esquire* and
Playboy):

   In adolescence, I had only to say "God," and I would
   think of my groin. God was lust to me, God was very much

like the image of the Devil offered to us by my good school, St. Matthew's. Chapel was daily and devoted to Christ, but once a week on average we might hear of the temptings of a somewhat legendary master-ghost named Satan. Chapel kept God and Satan well separated, but I, unlike other Matties, kept mixing them up. I had my reasons: I was introduced to carnal relations during my first year in the school by an assistant chaplain of St. Matthew's who *glommed*—I choose the word to convey the sensation of that rubbery indefatigable seal—my fourteen-year-old penis in his tight, unhappy lips.

We were in Washington, D.C., on a school trip. . . .

In an adventurous work this large we want "Call me Ishmael" for a first paragraph, something to conjure with. But this paragraph (which when it first appeared in *Esquire* I thought was the novel's first paragraph) seems at first merely shocking and clever. When we know more about the story and its people, we find the shock justly used and the paragraph daring rather than clever. With plenty to conjure with.

This novel is about the American soul, God, fear, dread, the CIA, and white Anglo-Saxon Protestants of a patrician order. The youth above, Harry Hubbard, is the godson of vastly respected Hugh Tremont Montague, a CIA panjandrum, code-name Harlot. Harry's own father was a founding member of that international network. Today Harlot may well be crazy. But as his name signifies, he is crucified upon a hill of pain—a Satan God needs to energize Himself. So in the first paragraph we get the ambiguities, "God was very much like the image of the Devil" and when Harry hears of "the temptings of a somewhat legendary master-ghost named Satan," he's hearing also about the CIA spook-master who is his godfather. And Harry had been deflowered at fourteen in the devil's playground, Washington, D.C., by an assistant chaplain of St. Matthew's. And Mailer seals the event in our imagination with graphic immediacy. The word *glommed* eloquently foretells much *spiritual* glomming that lies ahead. Mailer begins high, is clear enough to grip you, and is serious.

The next first paragraph is from the overture (as it appeared in *Playboy*):

> On a moonless night in March, returning to The Keep, I took the coast road from Bath to Belfast in Maine, the road that goes by Camden. In every cove was fog and it covered one's vision like a winding sheet, a fog more than worthy of the long rock shelf offshore where sailing ships used to founder. When I could not see at all, I would pull the car over; then the grinding of the buoys would sound as mournful as the lowing of cattle in a rain-drenched field. The silence of the mist came down on me. You could hear the groan of a drowning sailor in the lapping of that silence. I think you had to be demented to take the coast road on a night like this.

Masterful scene-setting. The self-revealing intimacy of the last line takes the curse off the high Gothic. That "winding sheet" should be retired but for its aptness about the drowning sailor, for it is Harry's spirit that is the mournful buoy, the lowing cattle in the rain-drenched field, the drowning sailor, and Harry wears the winding sheet. These things don't come to a man not spooked. And how well the paragraph's weight grinds down on *demented*, then drills it for shocks: "to take the *coast* road on a *night like this*."

For the record, here is *the* first paragraph of *Harlot's Ghost* as it finally appeared in volume one (volume two is still some years off):

> On a late-winter evening in 1983, while driving through fog along the Maine coast, recollections of old campfires began to drift into the March mist, and I thought of the Abnaki Indians of the Algonquin tribe who dwelt near Bangor a thousand years ago.

This is earlier in the same misty drive Harry was on when the fog forced him to stop and ask himself if he was demented to be taking the coast road on such a night. The softer opening here, not at all Gothic, gives us the long view of the land as it was when peopled by earlier tribes, who relaxed around their campfires long before the mind of America scurried with busy agents of the CIA. Paragraphs rich with awesome natural beauties follow. Long centuries of cornplanters, and braves and squaws in birchbark canoes, people musky with old sorrows and pleasures, become the Edenic backdrop for a demonized landscape Harry is about to fill in for us. These paragraphs infect us slowly with Mailer's theme and get one breath beating between reader and writer. They speak clearly and seriously and in their eloquence call upon the Muse to help him at his epic purpose and keep him equal to his subject. Some notes of melodrama in the overture may strike us as more from Verdi or Shakespeare than Tolstoy, but I suspend judgment for now. For me, volume one is a homer still flying out of the park.

Now for one of Mailer's larger influences, whom we'll get a fix on in three translations of the same great first paragraph:

> For a long time I used to go to bed early. Sometimes, when I had put out my candle, my eyes would close so quickly that I had not even time to say to myself "I'm falling asleep." And half an hour later the thought that it was time to go to sleep would awaken me; I would make as if to put away the book which I imagined was still in my hands, and to blow out the light; I had gone on thinking, while I was asleep, about what I had just been reading, but these thoughts had taken a rather peculiar turn; it seemed to me that I myself was the immediate subject of my book: a church, a quartet, the rivalry between Francois I and Charles V. This impression would persist for some moments after I awoke; it did not offend my reason, but lay like

scales upon my eyes and prevented them from registering the fact that the candle was no longer burning. Then it would begin to seem unintelligible, as the thoughts of a former existence must be to a reincarnate spirit; the subject of my book would separate itself from me, leaving me free to apply myself to it or not; and at the same time my sight would return and I would be astonished to find myself in a state of darkness, pleasant and restful enough for my eyes, but even more, perhaps, for my mind, to which it appeared incomprehensible, without a cause, something dark indeed.

—*Remembrance of Things Past* (1913–1927), Marcel Proust; translated by C. K. Scott Moncrieff and Terence Kilmartin, Random House edition 1981

Time was when I always went to bed early. Sometimes, as soon as I snuffed my candle, my eyes would close before I even had time to think, "I'm falling asleep." And half an hour later, wakened by the idea that it must be time to go to sleep, I would feel the desire to put away my book, which I thought I was still holding, and blow out the light. While I had been sleeping, my mind had gone on thinking over what I had just been reading, although these thoughts had taken an odd turn—I had the impression that I myself had turned into the subject of the book, whether it was a church, a string quartet or the rivalry between Francois I and Charles V. This conviction would stay with me for a few seconds after I woke; there seemed nothing irrational about it to my mind, but it lay like scales on my eyes and prevented them from realizing the candle was no longer burning. Then it would gradually become unintelligible, as the memories of a former life must be after a reincarnation; the subject of the book and myself parted company and I felt free to go on being it or not. Then all at once I would get back my sight and realize in amazement that I was in darkness, which my eyes found pleasant and restful enough

77

but which my mind enjoyed even more, seeing it as a phenomenon devoid of any cause and quite incomprehensible—what one might call being "in the dark," in fact.

> —Translated by James Grieve, Australian National University Edition, 1982

Time and again, I have gone to bed early. Often enough, my candle just out, my eyes would close even before I had time to realize, "I'm falling asleep." And half an hour later, the thought that it was time to go to sleep would wake me; I would try to put down the book which I believed was still in my hands and blow out the candle; still asleep, I would reflect upon what I had been reading, but such reflections took a peculiar turn, as if I myself had become what the book was about: a church, a string quartet, the rivalry between Francois I and Charles V. This notion would persist several seconds after I woke, and though nothing about it seemed irrational, it lay like scales upon my eyes and kept them from discerning that the candle was no longer lit. Then it would begin to grow unintelligible, like the thoughts of a previous existence after metempsychosis; the book's subject would withdraw from me—I was free to deal with it or not; now I could see again, and I was amazed to find a darkness round me soothing to my eyes but perhaps even more so to my mind, which found it causeless, unaccountable, dark indeed.

> —Translated by Richard Howard, 1988

Proust cares not only about *what* happened in the past, but even more about how it felt to be there, what it smelled like, sounded like, tasted like, looked like. His strengths are physiological realism as an underpinning for psychological musings and his staggering architecture. As with James Joyce's *Ulysses*, crisis and face-to-face accusations and proofs don't interest him. Perhaps one of Joyce's unmeant, but closest, likenesses to Proust is his Gerty MacDowell chapter, a parody of the popular romance, in which at evenfall, Mr. Bloom stands musing on the girls on the strand and is lost in memory while he masturbates in his pants. Nothing happens, but there is a long discharge and release.

From the first paragraph you might think that this is the story of a man who can't get to sleep, and as you read, who can't get to sleep in Paris, in Combray, in Balbec, or even in Venice. But sleep is only the sliphorn by which the storyteller recovers his past; it stands for the artist's alpha state as he reawakens lost time, drawing from it materials for his rebirth, the rebodying in words of his own physiological, emotional, and artistic history. Dead loves are not dead, nor are dead enemies. Great drama and glittering dialogue await you as you enter Proust's repicturing of a society already lying in far-off mist as he writes. As we know, he wrote the end pages of the last novel first, where all the characters have aged, fallen into decay, or risen from commonness to social heights. So the time recovered is doubly far-off when we add to it the twenty-some years spent writing his book. He had given up ever being an artist when the theme of time recaptured struck him, the possibility of using the physiology of memory to bring forth sublimity, to remake himself in a body of words, and to lift sexual release—the lost loves, the kiss from Mama, the agony of never becoming one being with a loved one—into a long aesthetic release that is deathless. The blissfully unintelligible half-world of sleep, the alpha state, only seems unintelligible. It is actually a dictionary of the senses by which the Muse makes herself a new garment of words.

What Mailer borrows from Proust for *Harlot's Ghost* is the method. Instead of the small cake dipped in tea that brings Marcel's past back into physiological focus, Mailer uses a lost civilization in his first paragraph, and later sex, fear, dread and guilt will be the mainspring for his musings throughout. He rarely presents the action *now*. His storyteller muses, chapter by chapter, on the past and scenes are rendered less as great clashes than as moral and spiritual eddies and whirlpools at a remove from action: He tells how it tasted morally, felt spiritually, and dramatizes what, for him, is a physiology of soul, in this case, the American soul.

And please note *Ancient Evenings'* first paragraphs in light of Proust's "Then it would begin to grow unintelligible, like the thoughts of a previous existence after metempsychosis . . . a darkness . . . causeless, unaccountable, dark indeed." (Howard)

Proust's universe has its cosmic center in the mind of a dreamer, to whom all sensation—and all the folk who walk the country lanes, Paris boulevards, and live in the apartments of his unconscious—rises again glowing with blood. His first paragraph starts in bed with candlelight sinking him back into his mother's womb where he lies afloat on desire. *She* waits just off-stage with the kiss of peace. He is heavy and wordless and the candle he has snuffed still burns in the rooms of his brain. Where is he? He is in the navel of his wordless physiological history, the mystic, sensual center, awaiting rebirth—as a book! "I myself had turned into the subject of a book." (Grieve) The originality of this device hardly varies from that of Alice following *her* anxieties—the White Rabbit—down a rabbit hole into Wonderland, where she nearly drowns in her own tears, the Duchess cries, "Off with her head!", babies turn into piglets, and all things are mad as the March Hare. The device grants the storyteller godlike freedom. I pass through stone like a ghost. The one condition I place on myself is that all things must have feeling. Each detail must in some way be sensuous, if not to the body, to the sympathies—even Time, which I watch trace itself in the aging of faces. "No doubt my books too, like my fleshly being, would in the end one day die. . . . Eternal duration is promised no more to men's works than to men." (Andreas Mayor, *The Past Recaptured*)

He sounds his themes on the anvil of the first paragraph and sets out in search of lost time. Heroic invalid!

And here is the same first paragraph but in a Joycean variation:

riverrun, past Eve and Adam's, from swerve of shore to
bend of bay, brings us by a commodius vicus of recirculation
back to Howth Castle and Environs.

Sir Tristram, violer d'amores, fr'over the short sea, had
passencore rearrived from North Armorica on this side the
scraggy isthmus of Europe Minor to wielderfight his
penisolate war: nor had topsawyer's rocks by the stream
Oconee exaggerated themselse to Laurens County's gorgios
while they went doublin their mumper all the time: nor
avoice from afire bellowsed mishe mishe to tauftauf
thuartpeatrick: not yet, though venissoon after, had a
kidscad buttended a bland old isaac: not yet, though all's
fair in vanessy, were sosie sethers wroth with twone
nathandjoe. Rot a peck of pa's malt had Jhem or Shen
brewed by arclight and rory end to the regginbrow was to be
seen ringsome on the aquaface.

The fall (babbadalgharaghtakamminarronnkonnbronnton-
nerronntuonnthunntrovarrhounawnskawntoohoohoordene-
nthurnuk!) of a once wallstrait oldparr is retaled early in
bed and later on life down through all christian minstrelsy.
The great fall of the offwall entailed at such short notice
the pftjschute of Finnegan, erse solid man, that the
humptyhillhead of humself prumptly sends an unquiring one
well to the west in quest of his tumptytumtoes: and their
upturnpikepointandplace is at the knockout in the park
where oranges have been laid to rust upon the green since
devlinsfirst loved livvy.
                                —*Finnegans Wake* (1939), James Joyce

Just as Proust slips into layers of unintelligibility and finds
he's become a book in the dark, so Joyce slips into his book
of night and finds the English languish gone pftjschute,
buttended and bellowsed. It's had a great fall and rot a peck

of pa's malt will sensify its scraggeration or give us a penny-worth of rainbow in resolving its recirculations. Let all hope be laid to rust on that scour, my gorgio. It's helpless. You'll not do it. You're not meant to, you humptyhillhead. Have a great fall, Dumpty? And avoice from afire cries, All the king's men can't put my languish together again!

It's the Wall Street crash. It's the Fall. It's Humpty Dumpty split like an egg. It's Finnegan tottered from a latter into the landscape.

My feeling, after forty years with this book, is that it's not meant to make soundsense, nor even as much sense as Joseph Campbell and Henry Morton Robinson's *A Skeleton Key to Finnegans Wake* tries to lend it. Here is *The Evening World*, to be read on your pillow, where litterish fragments lurk dormant. Just don't force logic where none is meant. It's sleep, it's night. Jump in.

The *Wake* is a stirring work of lyric screwiness. Adam and Eve as a "wallstrait oldparr" whose Fall, the market crash of '29, "is retaled early in bed and later on life down through all christian minstrelsy" I find funny when I stop to listen to it. Say it over with an Irish accent—but leave out the (bababa . . .) sound of the Fall: "The fall of a once wallstrait oldparr is retaled early in bed and later on life down through all christian minstrelsy." How was your Irish? Now, as amusing as I find my Wall Street reading, I don't know that it's what Joyce meant. He may mean a wallstrait oldparr, a pair of married Puritans strait as walls, who sinned. Who knows? We make what we can out of it. And the *Wake*, humbly dumbly, rises to high passion, falls worbbling with laughter, sings about woman with a whispering innerness that no other book can call on, not even *Ulysses*. If it ever makes sense to you, you're plobbicidal and should be removed. Joyce bent every arm on his body to deepen the *Wake*'s obscurity. It's not meant to have a form you can make out in the darkness. It's meant only to be climbed, to go whispering with into the hitherandthith-ering. *Night!*

I said in the beginning that "a writer has to be clear, has to get one breath beating in the ribs of writer and reader, and he must mean what he's saying." Does *Finnegans Wake* do any of this? Well, the writing has a clear lyric voice, I love "Sir Tristram, violer d'amores, fr'over the short sea" (the Irish Sea which Tristram crossed with Iseult, and whereon they took the love potion that led to her adultery and to the lovers' deaths, a variation on the fall of Adam and Eve and the wallstrait oldparr). I'm amused by the rich "pftjschute of Finnegan" (his chutelike fall that includes the phfft and whoosh of his fall); I'm in awe of the hundred-letter thunder of the fall, bababa . . . thurnuk; I enjoy "sosie sethers wroth" whoever that angry girl is, and I think the malt "brewed by arclight and rory end to the regginbrow was to be ringsome on the aquaface" is fabulous, meaning I would guess something about two sons of Noah (a noted drunkard) making whiskey by the ark's sacred light and taking dad to a roaring fall of the rainbow ringsome on the aquaface. I may be all wet—but Joyce is happy and tells me, "Go on, go on!" So I say Finnegan has fallen into the landscape, is so dizzy he can't find his tumpty-tumtoes, but his toes, or shoes, are the upturnpikepointand-place rising like steeples to the west. Which is followed by the knockout in the park, with boxer Finnegan counted out, and looking at his toes—along with Adam and Eve he's been knocked out of the garden. All this takes place in the tide-flow of a dreaming brain, with all the figures doubling their shadowroles—in the Muse's unconscious, at its most stutteringly eloquent. So, I make the case that Joyce gets one breath beating between his ribs and mine, and I know he means what he's saying although he smiles like a gorgio doublin his mumper—a snappy young Dubliner downing beers (just a guess—and likely a wrong one at that!).

riverrun, past Eve and Adam's, from swerve of shore to bend of bay, brings us by a commodius vicus of recirculation back to Howth Castle and Environs.

The first paragraph is one of the clearest sentences in *Finnegans Wake*, quite as mindbending, demanding and immediately eyebinding as one of Picasso or Bracque's most highly worked, yet instantly charming Cubist pieces. Something we can't quite make out shines through green shadows, and like a Cubist painting it clears up as we dig into its spell. The word placement and sinewy logic of the line, its springing *b*'s and hard *c*'s giving quiet muscularity, help make it an inspired lyrical utterance, human speech holding eternal light within it, like the flow and beat of Bach's "Jesus, Joy of Man's Desiring."

Let's go back to simpler English:

> Leo-Teddy under gas-blue Lake Erie sky where Daddy rows past the nightline searching for sturgeon. Gray waves and white glow on skyburning wave. Daddy, a whale! Teddy cries and the twins scream down at a sturgeon circling the rowboat. The long fish hovers by the oarlock while Durwood stands with the gaff. Quickly he drives pole under snout and hooks up through mouthroof and then five-foot whale beats in the boat white belly up and Durwood drives knife into heart and splits the fish in a stroke from throat to vent. Leo and Teddy gape at bowels slipping overboard and there in the wide cavity spills gleaming gray caviar. Daddy grins blissfully, rinsing his bloody blade in waves, and sheathes it. Stars rise on the watergardens. They row home, a red railroad lamp burning on the bow in the night.
> —*Sweet Adversity* (1978), Donald Newlove

Why do books die? Because the words go dead, if they weren't already lifeless when put down. The paperback *Sweet Adversity* embodies in one volume my hardback Siamese twin novels *Leo & Theodore* (1972) and *The Drunks* (1974). I had just finished the first draft of *Leo & Theodore* when I came upon a passage in *Ulysses* that made me stop revising and think hard. The passage showed Mr. Bloom judging a restaurant, should he have lunch there or not, and this is what Joyce wrote:

His heart astir he pushed in the door of the Burton restaurant. Stink gripped his trembling breath: pungent meatjuice, slush of greens. See the animals feed.

Men, men, men.

Perched on high stools by the bar, hats shoved back, at the tables calling for more bread no charge, swilling, wolfing gobfuls of sloppy food, their eyes bulging, wiping wetted moustaches. A pallid suetfaced young man polished his tumbler knife fork and spoon with his napkin. New set of microbes. A man with an infant's saucestained napkin tucked round him shovelled gurgling soup down his gullet. A man spitting back on his plate: halfmasticated gristle: gums: no teeth to chewchewchew it. Chump chop from the grill. Bolting to get it over. Sad booser's eyes. Bitten off more than he can chew. Am I like that? See ourselves as others see us. Hungry man is an angry man. Working tooth and jaw. Don't! O! A bone!. . . .

—Roast beef and cabbage.

—One stew.

Smells of men. Spaton sawdust, sweetish warmish cigarettesmoke, reek of plug, spilt beer, men's beery piss, the stale of ferment.

His gorge rose.

Couldn't eat a morsel here. Fellow sharpening knife and fork to eat all before him, old chap picking his tootles. . . . Scoffing up stewgravy with sopping sippets of bread. Lick it off the plate, man! Get out of this.

—*Ulysses* (1922), James Joyce (pp. 138–39)

What struck me about this was the power of Anglo-Saxon, every word a wriggling earthworm. Here was writing, stripped to the nerve ends. And checking it over, I found that aside from pallid and halfmasticated, which came from Latin, every word was Anglo-Saxon or had been used in English speech for at least three hundred years. The words in this passage—its poetic genius aside—would never go dead as long as English is spoken. And I began to sense everywhere the gangrene of Latin, words like discontinue for break off, continue for go on, multiple for many, permanent and durable for lasting or hard, impenetrable for dense, annual for yearly and so on, words that flattened sentences lifeless. A lightweight discovery, perhaps, but to me a sunburst. Joyce, of course, drew from all tongues. That was Joyce. I thought I saw for myself a foolproof way to turn words up to full power, and so I spent the next three months checking every word in my first draft for its roots and retonguing *Leo & Theodore* into Anglo-Saxon, and later did the same for *The Drunks*. Now you may say, But Donald, your title *Sweet Adversity* is from Latin! True, but sweet are the uses of adversity, Shakespeare tells us, and adversity has been in English use for over three hundred years. *Today* I'm not unbending about my fix on Anglo-Saxon. In Mailer's paragraph about God, lust and Harry Hubbard's groin in *Harlot's Ghost*, indefatigable rather than tireless is okay because its hard *g* empowers the eloquence of *glommed*. Joyce and Mailer sing as the Muse tells them. She tells me something else and has given me a song of my own. Such was my voice in the seventies. Twelve years later my voice was this:

> What could be more hopeless than a madwoman marrying a drunk? But cities have always been full of crazy people and alcoholics who marry. That lasting love can grow from such a union—such a fearful matching of cracks—is a miracle.
> —*Curranne Trueheart* (1984), Donald Newlove

Harold Brodkey kept readers waiting for two decades or more while writing *his* version of the Proustian novel. As seeming pieces of it appeared, the novel's fame grew and almost too much was expected from the finished work. Could it live up to its press as a work of high literary genius? Now the novel is here, in an incredible publishing month that found two literary giants going head to head with huge novels that bid to be the legendary Great American Novel, Mailer's long-awaited *Harlot's Ghost* and Brodkey's *The Runaway Soul*, which for readers was a demanding experience something like *WAR AND PEACE MEETS THE BROTHERS KARAMAZOV!*

Both novels have a startling likeness of method, taking off from the long look backward of *Remembrance of Things Past*, with no action happening Now. All arrives through a subjective veil. All three have an overture, a rhapsody to the Muse that gives the novel's highest pitch of eloquence and purpose. Set in 1930, Brodkey's overture is three supercharged paragraphs about his hero's birth. Here's the first paragraph:

> I was slapped and hurried along in the private applause of birth—I think I remember this. Well, I imagine it anyway—the blind boy's rose-and-milk-and-gray-walled (and salty) aquarium, the aquarium overthrown, the uproar in the woman-barn . . . the fantastic sloppiness of one's coming into existence, one's early election, one's senses in the radiant and raw stuff of howlingly sore and unexplained registry in the new everywhere, immensely unknown, disbelief and shakenness, the awful contamination of actual light. I think I remember the breath crouched in me and then leaping out yowlingly: this uncancellable sort of beginning.

Before I talk about this, let's read the first paragraph after the overture, set fourteen years later, in 1944, at 6:12 a.m.:

> Sometimes waking feels *piggish*: you know? Rooting and snuffling and snouting around? Do you think dreams are elegant? I do. I think they are—sometimes.

Anyway, sometimes it seems a shame to leave one's dreams. Maybe it's because real life is hard. I don't, as a rule, have strong opinions about those matters any more than, when I first awake, I know quite who I am or where I am; I don't remember what I am *supposed to look like*. The unfixity—well, I was adopted into a new family when I was two. Waking up was weird then. . . .
—*The Runaway Soul* (1991), Harold Brodkey

The second opening finds us familiarly in little Marcel's bed, but with Brodkey's storyteller, Wiley Silenowicz, waking up, not going to sleep. This famous setting is so *borrowed* that it's Brodkey's bow to the master.

Brodkey's earlier stories, which once seemed a part of *The Runaway Soul*, turned out to be mere charcoal sketches with a far firmer sense of story than the novel has, which tells of the hero's life *below the action* or *below the story*. Brodkey's relentless focus on Wiley's mental life makes for a dangerous novel—dangerous for Brodkey, in that thousands of readers will belly up like flies in a closed cabin—and dangerous for readers who go the distance, in that novels by other writers will seem half-empty without their authors' fingers plunging into the subconscious and puttering around on the brain pan as Brodkey's do. We become shockingly aware of what writers leave out to keep their stories moving. I foresee Brodkeyites swearing by his infrared sightedness in the dark.

I'd like to write about Brodkey's first paragraphs in Melville's admiring tones when he reviewed Hawthorne's *Mosses from an Old Manse*, which Brodkey may even deserve. But I'm not Melville, and anyway these paragraphs drive me stupid with nitpicking—much of which I've removed from the following comments, for my own sake.

The overture is pitched at the awesomely outsized and marvelous as we experience the birth of a prodigy. The hero later confesses he's a prodigy. If pushed, Wiley might even imagine the bonding of sperm and egg which gave him life ("I think I remember . . .") even as he can recall the taste of salt in the birth sac. Should we doubt his gargantuan molecular memory? Well, no. It's the novel's subject.

Even so, I find the style at odds with itself. "I was slapped and hurried along in the private applause of birth. . . ." Wiley is slapped into breathing and hurried along (from doctor to nurse?—or into Life itself, as in "Git along, little Wiley"?) to the private applause of birth. But I'm lost already. If he was slapped in the first phrase, why is he hurried along to be slapped again? Or is the private applause a restatement of the slap? I long misread this opening sentence to mean Wiley was hurried along in the womb and arrived at the private applause of his slap. I still wonder who's applauding—the doctor? maybe the adults in the room? What's so private about that? Is Wiley applauding himself? For me, this pretty sentence—like a Dylan Thomas line—has more music than sense to it. Which is okay! This is an overture.

Then we get ". . . the blind boy's rose-and-milk-and-gray-walled (and salty) aquarium, the aquarium overthrown, the uproar in the woman-barn. . . ." The blind boy is Wiley but he is also blind Cupid, or Eros, the root meaning of hero, who is one to be loved. And we see the little god against a rose-and-milk-and-gray wall, a Tiepolo cherub on sky blue. Then comes "the aquarium overthrown, the uproar in the woman-barn. . . ." Woman-barn is marvelous, though I long misread it to mean Wiley presenting in the breech and creating an uproar even before he was slapped. But no, woman-barn must suggest the swollen belly, not the womb agape. For me—just for me!—the thought of an aquarium gushing from a woman-barn feels forced. And a baby in a tank in a barn seems outlandish, although "uproar" does underscore Wiley's fantastic passage, as does "the fantastic sloppiness of one's coming into existence. . . ." But at once I'm thrown another curve, "one's early election. . . ." "Election" stops me dead as I sound the range of meanings in the word and try to choose the most apt. Should I skip over election, as well as asking what agency is doing the electing—Wiley, his parents, nature, or God and the angelic hosts? Anyway, Wiley is registered "in the new everywhere. . . . the awful contamination of actual light." Contamination holds overtones of Original Sin, and Wiley is a wily prodigy from his uncancellable first breath. I like the paragraph turning at last on three legalisms: election, registry, uncancellable. Wiley has been delivered into the Law.

Phrases of intense originality leap out of this paragraph and overcome my nitpicking. The good parts are so good, the energies so strong, that I don't care if—for me—sense fades in and out. I hear this paragraph in part as music, in part as poetry, and so smartingly fresh that "the awful contamination of actual light" pulls hairs from my arm and leaves pale bare skin.

The other paragraph opens with the underside of the first paragraph's high seriousness. "Sometimes waking feels *piggish*: you know? Rooting and snuffling and snouting around." Following the fireworks of Wiley's birth, Brodkey sucks us in with a quiet moment. We are offered piggishness as a way of thinking about waking up. I admit I've heard myself snoring in a chair and wakened myself because I sounded piggish. But then Wiley asks, "Do you think dreams are elegant? I do. I think they are—sometimes." Well, once more I long misread this to mean that the waking pig was snuffling after dreams as if dreams are truffles. Now I think he means that dreams are sometimes elegant, but the pig who dreams them isn't. No man sleeps elegantly. I hear Wiley on pigs and on the elegance of dreams as two voices yoked by violence. For me, the paragraph grinds away at something not quite brought to light. The real subject of the paragraph is that Brodkey makes clear he's going to take us down into the finest soul-tissues of his hero—however vulgar or fey they may be—but that we will not be warmed by the lens, and rarely by what we see.

The Runaway Soul is an exacting work of great genius whose art can tire you. Someday I may find its art altogether exciting. *Moby Dick* and *Ulysses* once put me to sleep. Now they keep me awake. Great talents can keep you awake round the clock. Genius does what it must and waits for you to grow up to its interests.

Here's the most famous first paragraph written by any American, so let's ask this voice some questions:

> Call me Ishmael. Some years ago—never mind how long precisely—having little or no money in my purse, and nothing particular to interest me on shore, I thought I would sail about a little and see the watery part of the world. It is a way I have of driving off the spleen, and regulating the circulation. Whenever I find myself growing grim about the mouth; whenever it is a damp, drizzly November in my soul; whenever I find myself involuntarily pausing before coffin warehouses, and bringing up the rear of every funeral I meet; and especially whenever my hypos get such an upper hand of me, that it requires a strong moral principle to prevent me from deliberately stepping into the street, and methodically knocking people's hats off—then, I account it high time to get to sea as soon as I can. This is my substitute for pistol and ball. With a philosophical flourish Cato throws himself upon his sword: I quietly take to the ship. There is nothing surprising in this. If they but knew it, almost all men in their degree, some time or other, cherish very nearly the same feelings towards the ocean with me.
>
> —Moby Dick (1851), Herman Melville

Great writing is dangerous to the writer as well as the reader. This novel killed Melville in the book trade. He took off his mask as the happy-go-lucky seafarer and let his nerves show from head to foot and was shot dead in the market. Moby Dick sold about twenty-five hundred copies in its first seventy years after seeing print. At thirty-two, Melville was eaten alive by failure, never regained his once large body of readers, and, after two more failed novels, had to go to work as a lecturer, and later as an outdoor customs inspector. Life as a novelist ended.

Moby Dick feels written by a man taking a fabulously powerful horse out for a canter and leaping stone walls in the April mist. This horse can beat any creature on earth for speed and muscularity, and Melville, writing at thirty, feels its blood energies ablaze in his brain. I can write *anything*! To see how dangerous this book was, remember that it came out thirty-three years before the darkness and scorn of *Huckleberry Finn* and ten years before the massacres of the Civil War, when the American people were largely country folk and read Emerson on self-reliance, nature, and the Over-Soul, if they could stay awake past nightfall. Today, in light of the White Whale's fame, we tend to read the opening as if it were tiresome scene-setting we must read before the good stuff starts. We don't read Melville's opening as he meant it to be read. What is Melville saying here? He speaks with a pessimism not heard since Shakespeare's *Timon of Athens*, with charcoal darks not used since *Hamlet* (1602) and *King Lear* (1605), and not picked up as deeply again until Louis-Ferdinand Celine's *Journey to the End of the Night* (1932). Melville, at thirty, is in his graveyard period, the same night that carried Shakespeare at thirty-six through Hamlet's suits of solemn black and chats with a skull.

Ishmael tells us he's an outcast and that his story begins some years ago—he dismisses telling us just when, only that he was broke, had lost interest in land, and thought he would go to sea. He'd been getting angry too often and had high blood pressure. His face had grown grim, he was depressed and eyeing coffin warehouses with helpless interest. He was stepping into the trains of funerals of people he'd never met, chronically morbid, in fact, so overwhelmed with black thoughts that he wanted to punch people's hats off to wake them up to the horrors of the world. It's time for getting to sea, fast, rather than shooting himself or doing himself in with a sharp instrument. It's not surprising that he needs the ship-cure. All men feel the ocean can save them from themselves—if they're not in Crane's open boat on heavy seas.

This is not "The Legend of Sleepy Hollow" (1820)!—not the blithe diet Americans were used to, despite the jokiness behind Ishmael's learned high style. Is Melville speaking directly to us? No. Ishmael is, as well as he can, and Melville speaks through his mask as this sour-voiced, seagoing schoolmaster. But it is this sour mask that allows Melville to split open the pet American beliefs in free will, foreordainment by God, the need for those spine-stiffening virtues lauded by Emerson's essays, and in the guilt, hellfire and damnation painted into men's minds by the Puritans. Melville cleared his throat deeply before daring to write *Moby Dick*'s first paragraph, then assigned it to Ishmael instead, with his quiet scorn for cities, and for blind innocence.

A note: All the feelingful words in this paragraph—the dismissive "never mind," the driving off, growing grim, a damp, drizzly November in my soul, knocking people's hats off, all men cherish—are Anglo-Saxon. Even cherish is Middle English. The only three words I think would better the paragraph are helplessly for involuntarily, carefully for deliberately, and one by one for methodically. Deliberately and methodically make a mouthful in one sentence anyway, when we want the reader falling through this paragraph as if stepping off a pier while reading.

Marguerite Young's *Miss MacIntosh, My Darling* (1965) is a lost American classic that has had two rebirths, three deaths, and may be striving to rise again. It starts:

> The bus-driver was whistling, perhaps in anticipation of
> his wife, who would be a woman with ample breasts, those
> of a realized maturity. It would be impossible that he did
> not have, from my point of view, a wife and children,
> indeed, a happiness such as I could not imagine to be real,
> even like some legend out of the golden ages. He had

spoken numerous times during our journey of his old woman waiting, and he was going home.

As if he were a Jehovah's Witness or a member of some other peculiar religious sect, his bushy hair grew almost to his shoulders. A Witness would not perhaps drive a Grey Goose bus, even in this far country, this interior America, but his head was large, bulging, an old, archaic dome of curled sculpture, and his eyes shone with gleamings of intensified, personal vision. He drove, in fact, erratically, perhaps because of the heavy mist which all but blotted out the asphalt road, the limitation, and more than once, with the bus's sudden lurching, I had feared that we might veer off into a ditch, that himself and his three passengers would be killed, our dismembered heads rolling in a corn field of withered corn stalks. He had whistled with each new escape, had turned and smiled back over his shoulder with a kind of serene triumph, even when the bus had brushed against the sides of a lumbering moving van with furniture piled up almost to the low sky, an upright piano, a rocking chair, a clothes' horse, a woman's feathered hat bobbing at the top in the grey mist like some accompanying bird.

—*Miss MacIntosh, My Darling* (1965), Marguerite Young

I love the fun of this opening, the stepping into the mind of the drunken Jehovah's Witness bus driver, his openhearted guzzling and whistling as he lurches off the road, his bushy hair almost to his shoulders and large, bulging, archaic dome and eyes gleaming with intensified, personal vision, his veering away from ditches and whistling with a kind of serene triumph at each new escape, while worrying about his wife's taking his head off when he gets home. This is a disarming opening to a novel whose 1,198 pages in hardcover may give us the shakes upon weighing it as a possible read. But length is less of a hurdle than its driftiness as it swims here and there with the reader seeking a rock to stand on in its unfolding marvels.

I recently had the chance of asking Marguerite, a fellow

Villager here in Manhattan, about her first paragraphs. My questions went like this: What Muse or goddess—perhaps Isis?—did you have in mind in the first sentence about the "woman with ample breasts, those of a realized maturity"?

"I was thinking about his old woman," she said, "his wife."

"Hm, well, you suggest 'some legend out of the golden ages,' and he's carrying us into 'this far country, this interior America,' which is like some huge fictional world we're about to enter."

"It's not fictional to me."

"Just legendary? I mean, we're into 'a heavy mist' and twice you mention the possibility of severed heads, of 'our dismembered heads rolling in a corn field of withered corn stalks' and his guessing that the old woman 'would certainly take his head off.' Severed heads have a long metaphysical tradition of standing in for madness, the writer as a bodiless head the Muse speaks through, a kind of open sesame to the imagination, to heightened speech. Aren't you granting yourself all this with these suggestive images?"

"Good God, no."

"Now, Marguerite. Isn't this opening a prism through which we foresee the novel's themes? I look at the lumbering moving van passing by, with furniture piled up, and upright piano, a rocking chair, a clothes' horse, a woman's feathered hat bobbing at the top in the grey mist like some accompanying bird. That hat and feather, aren't those foretelling us about bald Miss MacIntosh, that sad masterpiece of red wig and false teeth and false breast, with her stout salmon-colored corset, old mackintosh, black umbrella, weird hats and white fur ear muffs?"

"*Ha!* It's a hat with a feather."

"But that jumble of furniture, the rocking chair, the piano, the clothes' horse, isn't each piece symbolic of—"

"Of nothing. I *say* what I mean. If something means more than what it looks like, I'll tell you."

"Well. Thank you."

What you see here is the mind of a writer raised in the forties and fifties on the study of lyric verse in such books as *Understanding Poetry* by Robert Penn Warren and Cleanth Brooks, with deeper study of T. S. Eliot, Wallace Stevens, Ezra Pound, Hart Crane and like mindbenders, with whom a word not only meant what it said but said much more. Among writers I am familiar with, the short poem, whose fragrance and meanings mingled in the mind with a sense of the unsayable, came first. Year after year, I read or scanned well-wrought criticism packaged by university footservants. How could mere prose, a story or novel, ever rise to the demands of verse? I feared the sword of these archangels of the English lyric, and sought foolproof wordhandling as they looked down on my scratchings. Criticism became an addiction. You see me above, wringing symbols from sentences where none are meant, and being brought to my senses by Marguerite.

All this I tell you because you may think *Miss MacIntosh, My Darling* a steep, fearful mountain of metaphysics. It isn't. Word by word, it's just what it says it is.

What first paragraphs do is make familiar the manner in which the book will tell itself, a manner which sometimes becomes the matter. We find the storyteller not quite sure about what she's telling us. *Is* the driver a Jehovah's Witness? Does he have some legendary, unimaginable happiness? The storyteller is ready to leap in and invent all that for him. She foresees the three passengers killed, and goes on about it graphically. Is the driver, after all, a bachelor? if so, some mad Don Quixote, a virgin spirit—"and his family life, an emanation of my over-active imagination, really, my desire for established human relationships?" The novel's largest theme is the split between illusion and reality, and it endlessly wreathes its illusion with details blooming out of details into dynasties of details, mystical rhapsodies, relentless catalogues and inventories. The wonderful humor of the half-drunken bus driver with eyes of intensified personal vision, singing, whistling, talking to himself, alerts us to the likelihood that there will be much more of the same fun—and there is!

> It was late afternoon, with heavy silver clouds which looked bigger and wider than cotton fields, and presently it began to rain. Big round drops fell, still in the sunlight, on the hot tin sheds, and stained the white false fronts of the row of stores in the little town of Farr's Gin. A hen and her string of yellow chickens ran in great alarm across the road, the dust turned river-brown, and the birds flew down into it immediately, sitting out little pockets in which to take baths. The bird dogs got up from the doorways of the stores, shook themselves down to the tail, and went to lie inside. The few people standing with long shadows on the level road moved over into the post office. A little boy kicked his bare heels into the sides of his mule, which proceeded slowly through the town toward the country.
>
> After everyone else had gone under cover, Miss Clytie Farr stood still in the road, peering ahead in her near-sighted way, and as wet as the little birds.
>
> —"Clytie" (1941), *Collected Stories*, Eudora Welty

This story is a failure, written in 1940 when Eudora Welty was thirty-one, and yet its handful of superb passages include what is arguably the best opening paragraphs she ever wrote. The scene-setting of the unpaved main street of Farr's Gin, the heavy silver rainclouds mirroring the cotton fields below, the hot tin sheds, white false fronts of stores, the alarmed chickens in the road, the dozing bird dogs caught in the first drops and shaking themselves down to the tail, the late afternoon shadows showing that the sun slants under the rainclouds, the people stepping into the post office not to get wet, and the bareheeled boy kicking the sides of his slow mule walking through town toward the country, seem like shots for a movie about slow Southern life and, for me, are given the touch of genius by the birds flying down into the wet dust to take baths.

That happens in the middle of the paragraph and sets us up for the fulfilling rhyme of the birds' return in the second paragraph:

> After everyone had gone under cover, Miss Clytie Farr
> stood still in the road, peering ahead in her near-sighted
> way, and as wet as the little birds.

What mystery! Why is that woman standing in the rain? And what imagining we bring to her near-sighted figure. We see her caught by Welty with the angular immediacy of a Daumier caricature. Welty tells us only that the woman is "peering ahead"—but she has hooked us through the roofs of our imaginations.

The second superb set of passages is about faces. The woman in a trance in the rain has become estranged from reality by an obsession with the faces of townsfolk. Most people have this feeling now and then, when all social illusion vanishes from the human face and the eyes and nose and mouth all join horribly in a way you'd rather not think about. This alienation is not uncommon among drinkers and the mad, and was a much-loved effect Tolstoy would swat us awake with just before a suicide attempt—and Hamlet glows with alienation, most strongly in his speeches "What a piece of work is man" and the one to Yorick's skull. Welty, however, tries to make the effect bear too much weight in the plot, and something is missing when Clytie's obsession pushes her into the amazing act of drowning herself in a rainbarrel. By that time, though, we have been through a gallery of mad family members that seem a parody of Faulkner Gothic. We, too, are estranged and feel nothing at Clytie's death. Quite likely Welty felt nothing either, her last word and image being ironic—a sure way to sever the reader's feelings. But her effects during the suicide arise in a delirium of excitement:

. . . The rain barrel was full. It bore a dark, heavy, penetrating fragrance, like ice and flowers and the dew of night.

How's that for writing?

Dock's shoes on the rocks up the hill and his heavy breathing had shut out all sound so that it seemed a long while she had heard nothing, and Amos lay too still, not clawing at the blanket as when they had started. They reached the ridge top where the road ran through the scrub pine in sand, and while the mule's shoes were soft on the thick needles she bent her head low over the long bundle across the saddle horn, listening. Almost at once she straightened, and kicked the already sweat-soaked mule hard in the flanks until he broke into an awkward gallop. "I know you're tired, but it ain't much furder," she said in a low tight voice.

She rode on in silence, her big body hunched protectingly over the bundle. Now and then she glanced worriedly up at the sky, graying into the thick twilight of a rainy afternoon in October; but mostly her eyes, large, like the rest of her, and the deep, unshining gray of the rain-wet pine trunks, were fixed straight ahead of the mule's ears, as if by much looking she might help the weary animal pull the road past her with her eyes.

—*The Dollmaker* (1954), Harriette Arnow

I get a big lift from great writing. The above might not strike you at first as great—but it is. First, it helps to know that the big woman, Gertie Nevels, is holding baby Amos who is choking to death on mucus and vomit. Aside from the natural grayness of a rainy day, the scenery's grimness is heightened by Gertie's plight. Her grit is embodied in the flow of one-syllable words that take on the flat rhythm of hillside covered and trees passed. So read it again, knowing that Dock is her helplessly tired mule, feel the strain, strain, strain, and then the wonderful tightening of tension with:

> . . . but mostly her eyes, large, like the rest of her, and the deep, unshining gray of the rain-wet pine trunks, were fixed straight ahead of the mule's ears, as if by much looking she might help the weary animal pull the road past her with her eyes.

I fault only the logic of "Now and then she glanced worriedly up at the sky, graying into the thick twilight of a rainy afternoon in October", which has Gertie graying into thick twilight rather than the sky graying into twilight, and might better be said, "Now and then she glanced worriedly up at a sky graying into the thick twilight of a rainy afternoon in October. . . ." You may not agree. But—when translated into another tongue, a sentence should pass smoothly over, without tripping up a translator already reeling under dialects from Kentucky hill-country and the Detroit melting-pot.

The Dollmaker shows the dehumanization of hill folks who move to Detroit during World War Two to make money in the factories. Even Gertie's artistry with a whittling knife is cheapened, when a toy store asks her to mass produce her dolls and her husband Clovis buys her a jig saw for zipping out doll parts. Death and tragedy smash down. The final blow comes when Gertie axes her unfinished big cherry wood figure of Christ to be used for pieces for pre-sold dolls. This grim masterpiece ends on a tiny note of uplift, with all the downtrodden people Gertie knows seen as bits and pieces of Christ suffering a human existence. The suffering, however, will go on, as unrelieved as smoke billowing from Detroit's dark satanic mills.

In 1947 George wrote again to Myra, saying that now the war was well over she should come home and marry him. She wrote back from Australia, where she had gone with her two children in 1943 because there were relations there, saying she felt they had drifted apart; she was no longer sure she wanted to marry George. He did not allow himself to collapse. He cabled her the air fare and asked her to come over and see him. She came, for two weeks, being unable to leave the children for longer. She said she liked Australia; she like the climate; she did not like the English climate any longer; she thought England was, very probably, played out; and she had become used to missing London. Also, presumably to missing George Talbot.

For George this was a very painful fortnight. He believed it was painful for Myra, too. They had met in 1938, had lived together for five years, and had exchanged for four years the letters of lovers separated by fate. Myra was certainly the love of his life. He had believed he was of hers until now. Myra, an attractive woman made beautiful by the suns and beaches of Australia, waved goodbye at the airport, and her eyes were filled with tears.

George's eyes, as he drove away from the airport, were dry. If one person has loved another truly and wholly, then it is more than love that collapses when one side of the indissoluble partnership turns away with a tearful goodbye. George dismissed the taxi early and walked through St. James's Park. Then it seemed too small for him, and he went to the Green Park. Then he walked into Hyde Park and through to Kensington Gardens. When the dark came and they closed the great gates of the park he took a taxi home. He lived in a block of flats near the Marble Arch. For five years Myra had lived with him there, and it was here he had expected to live with her again. Now he moved into a new flat near Covent Garden. Soon after that he wrote Myra a very painful letter. It occurred to him that he had often received such letters, but had never written one before. It occurred to him that he had entirely underestimated the amount of suffering he must have caused in his life. But Myra wrote him a sensible letter back, and

George Talbot told himself that now he must finally stop
thinking about Myra.

—"The Habit of Loving" (1957), *Stories*, Doris Lessing

Can writing get more colorless? Not a word sings. Why is
that? Is Lessing out to show us something about George, that
he is himself colorless, and letting her voice be George?
George, it happens, is sixty and a well-liked man of the theater, a producer who at will can choose to put on shows. But
nine-tenths of the story is about George's flat spirit away from
the theater, as if Lessing is showing the bon vivant's spiritual
underwear. George goes untroubled by philosophical thought,
or yearning after the meaning of life, he thinks only of his
emotions. Part of him is dead, or was never alive. Lessing
never tells us just what's missing, but lets us mull it over
for ourselves. What she does is give us—at the story's more
passionate moments—George's heartbreak, the big soggy
heart he carries about, until at last he marries a minor actress
twenty-five years younger than himself, goes hopefully into
marriage and years later admits that his wife does not love
him. Like her much harsher, greedy sister, she saw a good
thing and grabbed it.

Here and there throughout the story we are told about
George's heart, which gets to be an interesting pump. Echoes
of Chekhov roll over us, the master of heartbreak and big
losers. But we never feel anything for the hero or his problem,
unlike the feelingfulness Chekhov arouses in us, and it must
be that Lessing feels nothing very deeply either, as if there's
nothing deep to feel. Her aims go elsewhere. Writing this
story at twenty-seven or so, she keeps a tight grip on her
opening, lays out every fact like a social psychologist turned
storyteller, and quickly draws us into her sketch of an aging
seducer going to seed. George has loved many and loved no
one, not even his first wife. Women are for sexual relief, a
kind of habit, and don't mean anything. With a self-centered
hero like that, whose acts of giving come too late and are for

a woman with no head for what he gives, a coming of wisdom will demand great storytelling skill to make us feel that our time with him was well spent. We want more than the relief of curiosity about what will happen next. What does happen is not enough. But perhaps Lessing could not grant her hero a Tolstoyan reversal of character, if she didn't believe in such reversals, or had never lived through one. Don't fake it, she warns herself—and doesn't.

> There is a certain place where dumb-waiters boom, doors slam, dishes crash; every window is a mother's mouth bidding the street shut up, go skate somewhere else, come home. My voice is the loudest.
>
> There, my own mother is still as full of breathing as me and the grocer stands up to speak to her. "Mrs. Abramowitz," he says, "people should not be afraid of their children."
>
> "Ah, Mr. Bialik," my mother replies, "if you say to her or her father 'Ssh,' they say, 'In the grave it will be quiet.' "
>
> "From Coney Island to the cemetery," says my papa. "It's the same subway; it's the same fare."
>
> —"The Loudest Voice" (1959), *The Little Disturbances of Man*, Grace Paley

This may be the most neatly packaged story in Grace Paley's first book of short stories. There have been only three books of stories (and one of verse) in thirty-two years—her works are not as the stars in number. This begins as a kind of tall tale about Jewish sixth-grader Shirley Abramowitz whose voice is louder than dumb-waiters booming, doors slamming, dishes crashing and, as we soon hear, can take the labels off of soup cans. But all this was when Mrs. Abramowitz was still alive. The whole street would groan for Shirley to be quiet, to no avail. And the street wisdom that forgives Shirley's loudness is quite funny—"In the grave it will be quiet," and "From Coney Island to the cemetery, it's the same subway; it's the same fare." There's not a false note anywhere. We're ready to see where this monstrous little loudmouth will take us.

In this story, little Shirley—whose parents arrived here fleeing a tyrant—stars as spokeswoman in a Christmas pageant at her grade school, groaning, *loudly*, "My God, my God, why hast thou forsaken me?"

Her mother calls Shirley's casting "a creeping pogrom"—and the story only gets funnier.

A second story in this collection, "An Interest in Life," shows Paley at her best:

> My husband gave me a broom one Christmas. This wasn't right. No one can tell me it was meant kindly.
>
> "I don't want you not to have anything for Christmas while I'm away in the Army," he said. "Virginia, please look at it. It comes with this fancy dustpan. It hangs off a stick. Look at it, will you? Are you blind or crosseyed?"
>
> "Thanks, chum," I said. I had always wanted a dustpan hooked up that way. It was a good one. My husband doesn't shop in bargain basements or January sales.
>
> Still and all, in spite of the quality, it was a mean present to give a woman you planned on never seeing again, a person you had children with and got onto all the time, drunk or sober, even when everybody had to get up early in the morning.
>
> I asked him if he could wait and join the Army in a half hour, as I had to get the groceries . . .
>
> —"An Interest in Life" (1959), *The Little Disturbances of Man*, Grace Paley

We wonder about that broom—asking ourselves is it funny or forced—and read on to find out. Much later, John explains to her, "A new broom sweeps clean. I got to get out of here. I'm going nuts." And he packs and leaves. To join what Army, Welfare asks. Try the Brazilian Army, she says, seriously, or the Mexican Navy.

This story deserves full surprise all the way, and I'll tell you nothing more. It's the best in the book.

"In Chancery"

London. Michaelmas term lately over, and the Lord Chancellor sitting in Lincoln's Inn Hall. Implacable November weather. As much mud in the streets as if the waters had but newly retired from the face of the earth, and it would not be wonderful to meet a Megalosaurus, forty feet long or so, waddling like an elephantine lizard up Holborn Hill. Smoke lowering down from chimney-pots, making a soft black drizzle, with flakes of soot in it as big as full-grown snowflakes—gone into mourning, one might imagine, for the death of the sun. Dogs, undistinguishable in mire. Horses, scarcely better; splashed to their very blinkers. Foot passengers, jostling one another's umbrellas in a general infection of ill temper, and losing their foot-hold at street-corners, where tens of thousands of other foot passengers have been slipping and sliding since the day broke (if this day ever broke), adding new deposits to the crust upon crust of mud, sticking at those points tenaciously to the pavement, and accumulating at compound interest.

Fog everywhere. Fog up the river, where it flows among green aits and meadows; fog down the river, where it rolls defiled among the tiers of shipping and the waterside pollutions of a great (and dirty) city. Fog on the Essex marshes, fog on the Kentish heights. Fog creeping into the cabooses of collier-brigs; fog lying out on the yards and hovering in the rigging of great ships; fog drooping on the gunwales of barges and small boats. Fog in the eyes and throats of ancient Greenwich pensioners, wheezing by the firesides of their wards; fog in the stem and bowl of the afternoon pipe of the wrathful skipper, down in his close cabin; fog cruelly pinching the toes and fingers of his shivering little 'prentice boy on deck. Chance people on the bridges peeping over the parapets into a nether sky of fog, with fog all round them, as if they were up in a balloon and hanging in the misty clouds.

Gas looming through the fog in divers places in the streets, much as the sun may, from the spongey fields, be seen to loom by husbandman and ploughboy. Most of the shops lighted two hours before their time—as the gas seems to know, for it has a haggard and unwilling look.

The raw afternoon is rawest, and the dense fog is densest, and the muddy streets are muddiest near that leaden-headed old obstruction, appropriate ornament for the threshold of a leaden-headed old corporation, Temple Bar. And hard by Temple Bar, in Lincoln's Inn Hall, at the very heart of the fog, sits the Lord High Chancellor in his High Court of Chancery.

Never can there come fog too thick, never can there come mud and mire too deep, to assort with the groping and floundering condition which this High Court of Chancery, most pestilent of hoary sinners, holds this day in the sight of heaven and earth.

On such an afternoon, if ever, the Lord High Chancellor ought to be sitting here—as here he is—with a foggy glory round his head, softly fenced in with crimson cloth and curtains, addressed by a large advocate with great whiskers, a little voice, and an interminable brief, and outwardly directing his contemplation to the lantern in the roof, where he can see nothing but fog. On such an afternoon some score of members of the High Court of Chancery bar ought to be—as here they are—mistily engaged in one of the ten thousand stages of an endless cause, tripping one another up on slippery precedents, groping knee-deep in technicalities, running their goat-hair and horsehair warded heads against walls of words and making a pretence of equity with serious faces, as players might. On such an afternoon the various solicitors in the cause, some two or three of whom have inherited it from their fathers, who made a fortune by it, ought to be—as are they

not?—ranged in a line, in a long matted well (but you might look in vain for truth at the bottom of it) between the registrar's red table and the silk gowns, with bills, cross-bills, answers, rejoinders, injunctions, affidavits, issues, references to masters, masters' reports, mountains of costly nonsense, piled before them. Well may the court be dim, with wasting candles here and there; well may the fog hang heavy in it, as if it would never get out; well may the stained-glass windows lose their colour and admit no light of day into the place; well may the uninitiated from the streets, who peep in through the glass panes in the door, be deterred from entrance by its owlish aspect and by the drawl, languidly echoing to the roof from the padded dais where the Lord High Chancellor looks into the lantern that has no light in it and where the attendant wigs are all stuck in a fog-bank! This is the Court of Chancery, which has its decaying houses and its blighted lands in every shire, which has its worn-out lunatic in every madhouse and its dead in every churchyard, which has its ruined suitor with his slipshod heels and threadbare dress borrowing and begging through the round of every man's acquaintance, which gives to monied might the means abundantly of wearying out the right, which so exhausts finances, patience, courage, hope, so overthrows the brain and breaks the heart, that there is not an honourable man among its practitioners who would not give—who does not often give—the warning, "Suffer any wrong that can be done you rather than come here!"
—*Bleak House* (1852–1853), Charles Dickens

This is Dickens at forty at the height of his powers, and was my first choice among first paragraphs for this book. My favorite opening! In this novel Dickens foretells Franz Kafka's *The Trial*, with the novel's main legal case, bound up in fog, stretching back for generations, with litigants who have blown their brains out waiting for a judgment. Such is Jarndyce vs. Jarndyce, borne on fog to become the most famous legal case in English literature, with fog its inner light. This, by the way, is the last we see of fog—it rains for the rest of the novel.

Here we have fact kindled with fancy, plain London mud with a Megalosaurus slouching up Holborn Hill, the lamps muffled by Mesozoic fog. At first we are drawn in by crisp tasty sentence fragments, that fire us instantly. Slowly the sentences build, fall into cadences, huge rhythms in themselves a legal brief of the weather, and we see that we are locked into a gigantic metaphor, the fog as life today under the Law. No escape. Man gropes from birth to death under the fogbound glory of strictures stretching from time without memory, back to the Megalosaurus. As in *The Trial*, this is the first given of birth. You come under the Law.

But not only the Law, for you are born into the universal mystery of London, a city famed for fogs touched with blasts from furnaces and mills, strange greenish hues, white seamists, and the majesty of the law mingles with the mystery of place. Dickens finds a bottomless inkwell ready for his pen. How his heart must have leaped when he lighted into his first draft and found all that mighty heart suddenly awake and waiting for him to ask for any part of it. He, of course, had covered the law courts as a young journalist, and we can believe that the London and Chancery that he shows us are long simmered in memory, perhaps in part no longer there as he writes, and that many fogs and muds and lost streets go into this homecoming with his heart and youth. And for all the care and revision that go into these paragraphs, he never loses his goal, to keep the reader thrilled with everyday mud and fog made vivid as if in light of a murder, a strangeness so alien it's familiar. One is abroad in Purgatory and fingering a corpse in the road. A great fraud has taken place on a human life. As he tells us later, the Thames "had a fearful look, so overcast and secret, creeping away so fast between the low flat lines of shore: so heavy with indistinct and awful shapes, both of substances and shadow: so deathlike and mysterious."

All his dead are with him as he writes of the living. It's

great to be forty and rich and a genius who marshals his time to perfection as he brings forth the first draft of a serial he will later shape to his heart's desire. He is in command of all his ghosts as he builds their memorial out of mud and fog. He will never be forty again, just as Melville would never again be thirty and writing *Moby Dick*, nor Shakespeare thirty-six and holding Yorick's skull in his mind's eye.

Strike that anvil with all you've got.

> "I believe in change," Mrs. Shackelford declared the instant the thermometer was out of her mouth. Her operation had been two days before. "To remain young in spirit, we must move with the times. My poor mother set herself against all change . . ." she continued in her silvery voice.
>
> Miss Wickes, one of the colored nurses who had just been introduced into the Southern University Hospital, stood reading the thermometer beside the sunny window; her elbow was at the exactly correct angle. She went then, on noiseless feet, in her white nylon uniform, and put the thermometer back into its tube of alcohol on the washstand. She opened the notebook she had brought into the room with her and recorded Mrs. Shackelford's temperature and pulse. She was severely handsome; dark; hair strained back into a neat bun, features aquiline and regular. She filled a metal basin with warm water and began methodically to give Mrs. Shackelford her bath in bed.
>
> —"The New Order" (1954), Nancy Hale; reprinted in *The Signet Classic Book of Southern Stories* (1991), edited by Dorothy Abbott and Susan Koppelman

Why is this here? I read it and felt like a flattened balloon. All the wind went out of me. This is a safe, well-intentioned, low-energy story that first appeared in *The New Yorker*. It's what I call fine arts, or pottery making. The qualities of its appeal are that it reads well, grows in an orderly manner, and, at the end, arrives at a safe, neat turn of character. These are basic cardboard for box-making.

I do admire how each detail about the methodical (even robotic) Miss Wickes shows her braced to be upstanding in the "new order" of colored nurses allowed into this Southern hospital, and sense the shock of her dark skin against the white nylon uniform—an implied shock, not stated. I'm not saying that the title, a parody of Hitler's Aryan theory (and jab at the old South's white supremacy) isn't witty, or that Nancy Hale did not go through some artistic agony to make this story (it looks quite studied), or that her two characters aren't alive before her. I'm sure she's writing at her best and most spirited. But this story strikes me as workaday storytelling that has nothing new to say, means to shake no one's deepest beliefs or judgments, and in no way demands to be lifted up and looked at more than any other pebble on the beach. If agreeably bland, voiceless, characterless stories about good manners, with some small enrichment of the reader by a well-poised turn of character, were the most excitement that storytelling offered, I think I'd have taken up jazz trumpet more seriously.

Standing amid the tan, excited post-Christmas crowd at the Southwest Florida Regional Airport, Rabbit Angstrom has a funny sudden feeling that what he has come to meet, what's floating in unseen about to land, is not his son Nelson and daughter-in-law Pru and their two children but something more ominous and intimately his: his own death, shaped vaguely like an airplane. The sensation chills him, above and beyond the terminal air-conditioning. But, then, facing Nelson has made him feel uneasy for thirty years.

The airport is relatively new. You drive to it off Exit 21 of Interstate 75 down three miles of divided highway that for all the skinny palms in rows and groomed too-green Bermuda grass at its sides seems to lead nowhere. There are no billboards or self-advertising roadside enterprises or those low houses with cooling white-tile roofs that are built by the

acre down here. You think you've made a mistake. An
anxious red Camaro convertible is pushing in the rearview
mirror.

"Harry, there's no need to speed. We're early if
anything."

—*Rabbit at Rest* (1990), John Updike

When I first read this, standing in a bookstore and having
read all the Rabbit Angstrom novels so far, I was bowled over.
Boy, he's really announced it, Rabbit's going to die. And I
admired this opening all the way home, rosy and warm with an
airplane foretelling Rabbit's death, and telling myself, perhaps
enviously, well done, John! Then I sat down and reread it.
Then I read it aloud. That's not very good, a damnable voice
told me. But I stood my ground, reading it aloud still again.
It did become a mouthful. Tan, the voice said, he means
tanned. True, I'd had to stop and make sense of tan, and then
of a tan crowd when he clearly meant a crowd of tanned
people. And a funny sudden sigh leaked from me.

What effect does that endless first sentence aim for? The
shock of foreseeing Rabbit's death and our own as one. We
are tied into Rabbit's deepest fear, first page, first sentence.
But despite the wonderful airplane, it's a fear felt through a
mass of detail that lessens the tie's force. Or does it? Do the
tan, excited post-Christmas crowd and the Southwest Florida
Regional Airport add to the force of fear by giving us a neutral
background against which the shape of death stands out? Perhaps it does, and Updike takes that chance.

But why is this post-Christmas crowd excited? Is a star
coming in? Or is this just a movie crowd, background figures
for Harry and his wife? We don't know. Would this sentence
read better as:

Standing amid the crowd at the Florida airport, Rabbit
Angstrom has a funny sudden feeling that what he has come
to meet, what's floating in unseen about to land, is not his

son Nelson and daughter-in-law Pru and their two children
but something more ominous and intimately his: his own
death, shaped vaguely like an airplane.

I leave it up to you. Updike has already made his choice. But
let's move on.

The second paragraph, I'd say, sets us up for Rabbit's anxieties. In the first sentence, the airport is relatively new, but
relative to what? To other airports? To Interstate 75? To the
highway landscaping? Well, it's meant to lead us back into
Rabbit's unease, since Exit 21 has no billboards or "self-advertising roadside enterprises" for three miles, and Rabbit wonders
if he's made the wrong turn. So relativity must apply to Florida
airport landscapes in general. Just a guess! But the next sentence, would it be better with less landscaping? Doesn't the
fanciness weaken our tie with Rabbit's anxiety? Would this be
a stronger paragraph:

> The airport is new. You drive to it down three miles of
> divided highway that seem to lead nowhere. There are no
> billboards, no roadside stores. No low houses with cooling
> white-tile roofs that are built by the acre down here. You
> think you've made a mistake. An anxious red Camaro
> convertible is pushing in the rearview mirror.

Now does this tie us into Rabbit's fears more strongly? More
darkly? Of course, it lacks Updike's trademark cadences—and
he *is* out for a big fish, the huge experience of all Florida going
into you like acupuncture needles, a kind of epic *Life Goes to
Florida* triple issue in which you must read all the ads, not just
scan the high-gloss color photography but read every word of
ad copy beneath while taking in the story part of the page.
What if we cut out all the landscaping that didn't awaken the
novel's spine and got the book down from five hundred and
twelve pages to four hundred? Would it perhaps have more

punch? Lift your feet off the canvas? Live longer? Well, Updike has made his choice, and I go with him, thankful that such an artist lives among us. His four Rabbit novels are triumphant Americana played against a tragic bass of cities dying. I wish them well.

Here is my favorite first paragraph in all of Updike, written in the full glow of his thirty-seventh year:

> Men emerge pale from the little printing plant at four sharp, ghosts for an instant, blinking, until the outdoor light overcomes the look of constant indoor light clinging to them. In winter, Pine Street at this hour is dark, darkness presses down early from the mountain that hangs above the stagnant city of Brewer; but now in summer the granite curbs starred with mica and the row houses differentiated by speckled bastard sidings and the hopeful small porches with their jigsaw brackets and gray milk-bottle boxes and the sooty ginkgo trees and the baking curbside cars wince beneath a brilliance like a frozen explosion. The city, attempting to revive its dying downtown, has torn away blocks of buildings to create parking lots, so that a desolate openness, weedy and rubbled, spills through the once-packed streets, exposing church facades never seen from a distance and generating new perspectives of rear entryways and half-alleys and intensifying the cruel breadth of the light. The sky is cloudless yet colorless, hovering blanched humidity, in the way of these Pennsylvania summers, good for nothing but to make green things grow. Men don't even tan; filmed by sweat, they turn yellow.
>
> —*Rabbit Redux* (1971), John Updike

That fluorescence clinging to pale men emerging from indoors, and all the gradings of winter light at the pretwilight hour set beside the summer light at that hour, and the wincing brilliance over baking curbside cars, the torn out buildings now showing newly seen rear entryways and half-alleys, and the barren lots now intensifying the cruel breadth of the light, friend, this deserves the Dickens Ribbon with *Bleak House* Rosette.

> They threw me off the hay truck about noon. I had swung on the night before, down at the border, and as soon as I got up there under the canvas, I went to sleep. I needed plenty of that, after three weeks in Tia Juana, and I was still getting it when they pulled off to one side to let the engine cool. Then they saw a foot sticking out and threw me off. I tried some comical stuff, but all I got was a dead pan, so that gag was out. They gave me a cigarette, though, and I hiked down the road to find something to eat.
>
> —*The Postman Always Rings Twice* (1934), from *Three Novels by James M. Cain* (1970)

Looks easy, right? What's so brilliant about this kind of writing? Just sensations, isn't it? But where others strive to show us the whole man, Cain allows that Frank Chambers's idea of telling us about himself is to suggest that he has fucked himself blind on Tiajuana whores for three weeks and now needs every wink he can get on the hay truck. His first impulse when getting rousted is to joke with the driver and his buddy throwing him off. His gag dies, but he gets a cigarette from them. Then looks for something to eat—and cheats a sandwich joint owner out of a meal. "Then I saw her. She had been out back, in the kitchen, but she came in to gather up my dishes. Except for the shape, she really wasn't any raving beauty, but she had a sulky look to her, and her lips stuck out in a way that made me want to mash them in for her."

This is not Proust or Updike. The pages flash by in a glare and by page one hundred it's all over. My God, it looks so easy! Why can't I write this and sell millions of copies and have four movies made from my one novel? All I have to do is listen to my cigarette-hungry lungs, my girl-hungry loins. This story writes itself on the end of your senses, don't it?

But . . . it just doesn't. Much, much thought went into this story, into its legal technicalities, and an eighty-thousand-word trial scene was cut in one rip of the pencil—not enough lust and hunger. Lust and hunger? Well-l, after Frank and Cora murder her husband Nick, the sandwich joint owner, they push his car with his body in it into a ravine, and Cora has to look beat up: "I began to fool with her blouse, to bust the buttons, so she would look banged up. She was looking at me, and her eyes didn't look blue, they looked black. I could feel her breath coming fast. Then it stopped, and she leaned real close to me. 'Rip me! Rip Me!' I ripped her. I shoved my hand in her blouse and jerked. She was wide open, from her throat to her belly." And then things *really* cook up.

Cain, of course, wants to show that he has more than one pencil, and two years later turns *Postman* inside out with *Double Indemnity*, by making the stakes in life insurance as strong a storypuller as lust and by upgrading his characters' wits and educations. It's the same Depression, even in 1936, but iron skies of unemployment don't bend over insurance agent Walter Huff or well-heeled Phyllis Nirdlinger, a serial killer in blue silk pajamas. Here's the opening:

I drove out to Glendale to put three new truck drivers on a brewery company bond, and then I remembered this renewal over in Hollywoodland. I decided to run over there. That was how I came to this House of Death, that you've been reading about in the papers. It didn't look like a House of Death when I saw it. It was just a Spanish house, like all the rest of them in California, with white walls, red tile roof, and a patio out to one side. It was built cock-eyed. The garage was under the house, the first floor was over that, and the rest of it was spilled up the hill any way they could get it in. You climbed some stone steps to the front door, so I parked the car and went up there. A servant poked her head out. "Is Mr. Nirdlinger in?"

"I don't know, sir. Who wants to see him?"

"Mr. Huff."

"And what's the business?"

"Personal."

—*Double Indemnity* (1936), from *Three Novels by James M. Cain* (1973)

My wife doesn't hear anything special in *The Postman*'s first paragraph but relishes the crazy California house and slippery talk of *Double Indemnity*'s opening. *Double Indemnity* grabs you right off, but, for me, lacks the stylistic shock and originality of *Postman*. Maybe *Postman*'s electric plainness—even the first-time-ever absence of he saids and she saids from dialogue throughout the entire work—has weathered too many years for her to feel its shock. That first paragraph *looks* like ten thousand other first paragraphs—but for me the voice is uniquely Cain's. I can't say the same for *Double Indemnity*—or couldn't until I became familiar with his plots; then by the first sentence alone I hear a voice uniquely Cain's. "I drove out to Glendale to put three new truck drivers on a brewery company bond, and then I remembered this renewal over in Hollywoodland. I decided to run over there." That flat businessman's voice full of tired details, "three new truck drivers on a brewery company bond," "this renewal over in Hollywoodland," strikes us with its great daring, as if it says I'm completely disinterested in whether you read this or not, I'm an insurance agent, here are the facts. Here's how I came to this House of Death . . . and our ears prick up.

Cain knows that, lurking behind his first sentence, fate is hard at work to ensnare his very clever, very intuitive, very unimaginative insurance agent as he goes out to renew an auto policy and steps into a snake's nest of blue pajamas, blood money and a shivery, adventurous lunge at trading in all his bonds and renewals for a ride on the gravy boat . . . with Phyllis. "She didn't have on blue pajamas this time. She had on a white sailor suit, with a blouse that pulled tight over her hips, and white shoes and stockings. I wasn't the only one that knew about that shape. She knew about it herself, plenty."

That's the voice. Declaring, flatly declaring, that, like Frank Chambers with Cora, he's being suckered by a woman worth dying for.

I enjoy the opening of Jack Kerouac's *On the Road* (revised and published in 1957), but less so than that of *Visions of Cody* (1951–1952), which he wrote after the first version of *On the Road*, but which was published in complete form only in 1972, after his death three years earlier. Though New Directions brought out some bits and pieces in 1960. Here's *On the Road*:

I first met Dean not long after my wife and I split up. I had just gotten over a serious illness that I won't bother to talk about, except that it had something to do with the miserably weary split-up and my feeling that everything was dead. With the coming of Dean Moriarty began the part of my life you could call my life on the road. Before that I'd often dreamed of going West to see the country, always vaguely planning and never taking off. Dean is the perfect guy for the road because he actually was born on the road, when his parents were passing through Salt Lake City in 1926, in a jalopy, on their way to Los Angeles. First reports of him came to me through Chad King, who'd shown me a few letters from him written in a New Mexico reform school. I was tremendously interested in the letters because they so naively and sweetly asked Chad to teach him all about Nietzsche and all the wonderful intellectual things that Chad knew. At one point Carlo and I talked about the letters and wondered if we would ever meet the strange Dean Moriarty. This is all far back, when Dean was not the way he is today, when he was a young jailkid shrouded in mystery. Then news came that Dean was out of reform school and was coming to New York for the first time; also there was talk that he had just married a girl called Marylou.

—*On the Road* (1957), Jack Kerouac

Does this have a familiar ring?—"I first met Dean not long after my wife and I split up. I had just gotten over a serious illness that I won't bother to talk about, except that it had something to do with the miserably weary split-up and my feeling that everything was dead." How about:

If you really want to hear about it, the first thing you'll probably want to know is where I was born, and what my lousy childhood was like, and how my parents were occupied and all before they had me, and all that David Copperfield kind of crap, but I don't feel like going into it, if you want to know the truth . . .

—*The Catcher in the Rye* (1951), J. D. Salinger

Or even closer:

You don't know about me, without you have read a book by the name of "The Adventures of Tom Sawyer," but that ain't no matter . . .

—*The Adventures of Huckleberry Finn* (1885), Mark Twain

Huck, of course, is about to tell us all about his adventures on the road, or the Mississippi River, just as Holden Caulfield goes on a three-day journey within New York City. Along with Sal Paradise, Kerouac's hero, all three storytellers enjoy the same kitchen-table chattiness in assuring us about what's important in their road stories and what isn't. With Huck what's important is not telling any stretchers.

Jack Duluoz, the storyteller of *Visions of Cody*, is more than chatty, he's tidal, his voice is uniquely his and stands out as a great original's, far more so than Sal Paradise's voice at its low-key fact-gathering:

This is an old diner like the ones Cody and his father ate in, long ago, with that oldfashioned railroad car ceiling and sliding doors—the board where bread is cut is worn down fine as if with bread dust and a plane; the icebox ("Say I got some nice homefries tonight Cody!") is a huge brownwood thing with oldfashioned pull-out handles, windows, tile walls, full of lovely pans of eggs, butter pats, piles of bacon—old lunchcarts always have a dish of sliced raw onions ready to go on hamburgs. Grill is ancient and dark and emits an odor which is really succulent, like you would expect from the black hide of an old ham or an old pastrami beef—The lunchcart has stools with smooth slickwood tops—there are wooden drawers for where you find the long loaves of sandwich bread—The countermen: either Greeks or have big red drink noses. Coffee is served in white porcelain mugs—sometimes brown and cracked. An old pot with a half inch of black fat sits on the grill, with a wire fryer (also caked) sitting in it, ready for french fries—Melted fat is kept warm in an old small white coffee pot. A zinc siding behind the grill gleams from the brush of rags over fat stains—The cash register has a wooden drawer as old as the wood of a rolltop desk. The newest things are the steam cabinet, the aluminum coffee urns, the floor fans—But the marble counter is ancient, cracked, marked, carved, and under it is the old wood counter of late twenties, early thirties, which had come to look like the bottoms of old courtroom benches only with knifemarks and scars and something suggesting decades of delicious greasy food. Ah!

The smell is always of boiling water mixed with beef, boiling beef, like the smell of the great kitchens of parochial boarding schools or old hospitals, the brown basement kitchens' smell—the smell is curiously the hungriest in America—it is FOODY insteady of just spicy, or—it's like dishwater soap just washed a pan of hamburg—nameless—memoried—sincere—makes the guts of men curl in October.

—*Visions of Cody* (1972), Jack Kerouac

He begins to lose it in the second paragraph. The y on "insteady" is not a misprint. *Visions of Cody* is all first draft and Kerouac wanted it published exactly as written, misprints and all. The voice in the second paragraph, after that splendid opening, is sad to read, and goes to a gargle on "it's like dishwater soap just washed a pan of hamburg"—not what he means—and going groggily sentimental on "—nameless—memoried—sincere—makes the guts of men curl in October." Why October? It's the first cold month in which men order hamburgs? Of course, it isn't. Wine and pot makes slipsh of the pen and men stupid.

What makes the first paragraph as wonderful as it is? It's well within Updike's powers today, though perhaps not in 1951-52 when he was nineteen or twenty, and as we see from "The Time of Her Time" (1958) it was not yet within Mailer's powers in 1951 though it soon would be should he choose to write in an intellectual half-light. Well, is Jack's rhapsody mere brainless beauty? Perhaps—but it strikes notes not heard since Thomas Wolfe's great set-pieces in *Look Homeward, Angel* (1929) and *Of Time and the River* (1935), and we find ourselves going homeward to bread blocks in old diners and seeking "the great forgotten language, the lost lane-end into heaven" that only the released lunchwagon poet can bring back (note: a lunchwagon is fixed in place and you go to it; a lunchcart can come to you). Jack breaks down language, spelling, grammar, and presses his palm against the past to impress a decal there he can apply to paper. He surrenders to his vision with a wholeheartedness no one in America could match. He never wrote better than his best passages here. But the worst pages are deadly.

At the same time his friend William Burroughs had set sail on a novel unlike anything ever published anywhere:

> I can feel the heat closing in, feel them out there making their moves, setting up their devil doll stool pigeons, crooning over my spoon and dropper I throw away at Washington Square Station, vault a turnstile and two flights down the iron stairs, catch an uptown A train . . . Young, good looking crew cut, Ivy League, advertising exec type fruit holds the door back for me. I am evidently his idea of a character. You know the type comes on with bartenders and cab drivers, talking about right hooks and the Dodgers, call the counterman in Nedick's by his first name. A real asshole. And right on time this narcotics dick in a white trench coat (imagine tailing somebody in a white trench coat—trying to pass as a fag I guess) hit the platform. I can hear the way he would say it holding my outfit in his left hand, right hand on his piece: "I think you dropped something, fella."
>
> But the subway is moving.
>
> "So long flatfoot!" I yell, giving the fruit his B production. I look into the fruit's eyes, take in the white teeth, the Florida tan, the two hundred dollar sharkskin suit, the button down Brook's Brother shirt and carrying *The News* as a prop. "Only thing I read is Little Abner."
>
> —*Naked Lunch* (1959), William S. Burroughs

This still comes at us bristling with the comet-like brio it first had in 1959. It's one of the few straightforward pages in *Naked Lunch*, which quickly means to unsettle and shake us up. Today the novel reads more easily than it once did but is still a rough trip. What we'd thought—from parts seen ahead in *Big Table*, a Chicago literary magazine—would be thrillingly high-powered turned out to be an overwritten fantasy about Burroughs's paranoia, told in lies folded into lies that keep the reader at bay and unable to draw out much else than Burroughs's paranoia. Like Lon Chaney's *Phantom of the Opera*, it's a story that needs a big vamping organ score. I never finished a page by page reading, but the novel doesn't demand that, you can read its chapters in any order. This is not a fancy construction meant to amuse and thrill a literary public. It's a man jamming out that very public while still telling a highly energized tale that keeps him high and happy—and what keeps him happy is running from the thought police, a pressing anxiety relieved only by spinning fanciful, horripilating stories for his beleaguered psyche.

The title was given to Burroughs by Jack Kerouac, who said it meant the long stare someone high gives to a piece of meat on a fork—in that meat you see the whole history of flesh. In some ways *Naked Lunch*'s strongest attraction is its title. The reader seems promised a work magnificently inventive but then faces a sealed-in series of set-pieces that refuse to invite his interest; from afar he watches a fireplace dancing with an inflamed drug burlesque. Big come-on, fast let-down. You tell yourself, This isn't going anywhere, he's just beating off and can't come. You surrender and read on and on and, at last, quite tired, shut the book, asking, Well! what was that all about? I don't dismiss it, it's what he had to write, and I'm willing to wait a few more years to see if it doesn't open up to me more fully. In many ways, I'm in love with the book and could spend hours standing up for its games and artistry. But it keeps saying, I'm a leper, don't get too close.

The first sentence drops a "which" after dropper ["crooning over a spoon and dropper (which) I threw away"] and disorients us as we speed with the mind of the junkie. An Ivy Leaguer—a man as out of touch with reality as the junkie, a guy all front who calls the nameless orange juice puller at Nedick's by his first name—holds the door for him. Behind the fleeing junkie a narc in a white trench coat hits the platform but can't make the door. Like the Ivy Leaguer, the narc must be a fag (or passing as one), and—in a white trench coat—quite out of touch both with reality and his job. That they are "fruits" and "fags" also counts against their sense of reality in the junkie's mind. So we are shocked into action, plunged into unreality, and locked into the junkie's universe. He goes on layering us with his superfactual unreality by telling us that the Ivy Leaguer has a two hundred dollar sharkskin suit, a button down Brooks Brothers shirt, white teeth, a Florida tan, and carries *The News* for disguise (*The News* is meant to blur his fruitness and make him look straight—real fruits read *The New York Times*, while *The News* is for he-men who know the Nedick counterman's first name). We reel under the details of the false fag and are further disoriented by the grammar of "I look . . . take in teeth, tan, suit, shirt and carrying *The News* as a prop." There should be a *he's* or *his* before "carrying *The News* as a prop." As we read we don't notice the slip but do feel a muddying effect, whether Burroughs meant it or not. Perhaps he means it all to be read aloud, fast. It's hard to say what Burroughs means, since he's so poorly edited: aside from slips of grammar, Brook's Brother should be Brooks Brothers and Little Abner Li'l Abner. There's something unfelt or fake about "Only thing I read is Little Abner." Or is the use of "Little Abner" a joke to show how out of it the Ivy League (false?) fruit is? I think the junkie's heart would be racing, he'd be *telling himself* Straighten out, asshole! and far from spitting a tough-guy parting shot at the narc he'd be hyperventilating and thanking God the closed doors saved him from being caught. But we aren't into the *real* world of addiction (Burroughs had already done that in his 1953 Ace paperback *Junkie*), we're into a slangy mockup of the addict's fears, fantasies, babble and smart talk, packaged in a chaotic burlesque which warns the reader that *he* is just as degraded by huge mindfucking forces working upon him as the junkie is by junk. When Burroughs wrote this, his work was as dangerous as Melville's black humor in *Moby Dick,* *Pierre* and *The Confidence Man,* a trio whose morbidity killed him as a novelist. Part of the danger lay in Burroughs giving homosexuals a new hero, the junkie faggot cutting a revolutionary figure as he undermines society's thought police, and in being a writer fearlessly naked but whose work could now be dismissed as silly gay ravings. But Burroughs paid psychically for his daring, and the year after he finished writing *Naked Lunch* he calls the worst of his life, with the thought police and strange viruses swarming in on him. *Naked Lunch* had held them off. Now he was alone.

> A screaming comes across the sky. It has happened before, but there is nothing to compare it to now.
> It is too late. The Evacuation still proceeds, but it's all theatre. There are no lights inside the cars. No light anywhere. Above him lift girders old as an iron queen, and glass somewhere far above that would let the light of day through. But it's night. He's afraid of the way the glass will fall—soon—it will be a spectacle: the fall of a crystal palace. But coming down in total blackout, without one glint of light, only great invisible crashing.
> —*Gravity's Rainbow* (1973), Thomas Pynchon

Gravity's Rainbow is an exercise in logical idiocy, a kind of marijuana dream for geniuses, and could be called *Son of Naked Lunch*—or even *Bugs Bunny on Broadway.* Its working title was *Mindless Pleasures* and Pynchon was asked to do better.

Once you find out what they're about, the powerful first paragraphs suck you in for a long go at a huge but not always rewarding wonderwork. Lyrical set-pieces, such as that of nighttime London awaiting a Christmas rocket bombardment (". . . listen: this is the War's evensong, the War's canonical hour, and the night is real . . . Advent blows from the sea, which at sunset tonight shone green and smooth as iron-rich glass: blows daily upon us, all the sky above pregnant with saints and slender heralds' trumpets . . ."), give you hope that the book will make more sense than it means to. But even with his new title Pynchon plays Burroughs's game of hide-and-go-seek with the reader—a game both he and Burroughs gave up in later works.

Gravity's Rainbow is stuffed with encyclopedic learning, physics and chemistry, secrets of alchemy and centuries-old evil plots, famous figures from movies and cartoons, and almost enough fun to shoot down any dumb leanings toward high seriousness—but at last it comes across as both serious and a giant black laugh at itself. Its greatest gift is for words, its largest flaw too many dull or feelingless pages. Feelings break down as characters drop out until by book's end I barely care about anybody, although I'm often awed by the writing. That a reader puzzles his way through seven hundred and sixty pages of exactingly fine writing that circles about a conspiracy that is never fully revealed asks a lot of us. The novel is a forcefully monstrous metaphor upon a Faustian evil that may destroy all of us—so what can you do in the face of that evil? Pynchon chooses to laugh while whittling blissfully away at his huge work.

"I was so fucked up while writing it," he told a friend while revising his first draft, written largely in Mexico, "that now I go back over some of those sequences and I can't figure out what I could have meant." I'm sure that while revising he found out what he meant, but I have more trouble. I fear the novel will end up an unread classic, sunk by its overgrowth of learning, much as Robert Burton's *The Anatomy of Melancholy* goes revered but unread under its grappling with every known field of knowledge in 1621 . . . despite its satire and mockery.

Well, all that out of the way, why quote the first paragraphs? Because I like them! They're amazing! They have a voice! What other novel starts with "A screaming comes across the sky. It has happened before, but there is nothing to compare it to now"?

For the first two pages a British Commando has a nightmare,

that he's down in a pitchblack subway helping people evacuate London—though if they can hear the German V-2 rocket screaming above them it's already too late. And the arches of the subway remind him of the Crystal Palace, a huge iron-and-glass structure built in 1851 to house a World's Fair of modern marvels which have now brought us to this very danger of the world smashing to bits. "Above him lift girders old as an iron queen, and glass somewhere far above that would let the light of day through. But it's night. He's afraid of the way the glass will fall—soon—it will be a spectacle: the fall of a crystal palace. But coming down in total blackout, without one glint of light, only great invisible crashing."

All that creepy glass about to fall around you in the blackness. Poe could not do better! And wonderful, half-silvered, green-stained effects lie ahead down in that subway. And it's all so clear, you are the barestripped nerves of a man hearing a bomb come down, perhaps on his head. A great opening—don't let my carping keep you back. Many magnificent pages spread out from that spike Pynchon drives into your fear-centers with his hammerbomb. Gird yourself. Jump!

> It was a queer, sultry summer, the summer they
> electrocuted the Rosenbergs, and I didn't know what I was
> doing in New York. I'm stupid about executions. The idea
> of being electrocuted makes me sick, and that's all there was
> to read about in the papers—goggle-eyed headlines staring
> up at me on every street corner and at the fusty, peanut-
> smelling mouth of every subway. It had nothing to do with
> me, but I couldn't help wondering what it would be like,
> being burned alive along your nerves.
> I thought it must be the worst thing in the world.
> —*The Bell Jar* (1963), Sylvia Plath

And with that, Sylvia Plath says hello to hell. And within months is wired up for the worst thing in the world.

When we first read this opening, we think Plath has overdone the Rosenbergs and electrocution. After all, this is only the story of a college girl who has won a Manhattan summer vacation as a junior editor with a big slick women's magazine, right? Well, Esther Greenwood knows something is wrong. She should be having the time of her life, only she feels numb and just bumping about. And Plath shows us what's wrong, dramatically.

At thirty-one, Sylvia Plath was already an admired poet when she wrote *The Bell Jar*, her only novel, and published it in England in 1963. But a month after it came out, she gassed herself in her kitchen oven, despite growing fame and two small children. She'd had the suicide attempt and mental breakdown she writes about in her novel, had parted from her husband, and was indoors a lot during London's worst winter in one hundred and fifty years. Power failed, heat came and went, pipes froze. She worried about hurting the people she wrote about in her just-published novel. While writing the novel, she'd had a miscarriage, an appendectomy, and given birth to a second child. And she was having another breakdown, marked by a huge rash of poems, fast-written, white-hot and often anguished. She was looking for a psychiatrist. A sinus infection struck. She had no help with her babies. She was alone and felt stripped of all human illusions. Life was meaningless. Her novel reminded her of its controlling image, of her hospitalization in which she saw herself as a dead baby in a bell jar.

All this lay ahead for the girl who felt numbed by the Rosenbergs's electrocution. By now it's legend. What's not a legend is mental breakdown, the strain of recovery and resources stretched thin. To sit in a sometimes unheated house in subzero weather and feel a new breakdown coming on, the peril of familiar things turning strange, familiar faces becoming shapeless and lacking, was, finally, to choke in broad daylight. Some people laugh at Sylvia, finding her last poems just too whiny. They joke about her death. But we all go when time's up—and her brightness burst.

Like her legend, her novel, too, is part fiction. But unlike most poets who take up fiction, Plath has dramatic sense and her first paragraphs sizzle. It's a sultry sizzle. But Esther is in the pan, frying and burning with the Rosenbergs. "It was a queer, sultry summer. . . ." My God, is that sexy. I can just hear those words roll out of her. The novel's first feelingful word, "queer," tells you everything. Sylvia's talking right to you. I got so queer that summer. I didn't know what I was doing. . . . I'm stupid. . . . The idea of being electrocuted makes me sick. . . . I couldn't help wondering what it would be like, being burned alive all along your nerves.

And if you want to know what it's like, she tells you—shock by shock by shock. "It must be the worst thing in the world, Don, don't you think? I mean, New York was bad enough, but in the middle of an electrocution too? I couldn't get them out of my mind! Hm? Are you listening?"

Sylvia, go on! I'm all ears.

She went on. And it turned out to be as dangerous as *Moby Dick* for Melville, *Naked Lunch* for Burroughs, or *To the Lighthouse* for Virginia Woolf. It was life-threatening, risky business. Plath puts it like this, ". . . I felt as though I were carrying [a] cadaver's head around with me on a string, like some black, noseless balloon stinking of vinegar."

When Sylvia starts digging down for that kind of stuff on page one and serves it up sultry and sizzling, she's way, way out on the thinnest ice—very dangerous place to be, with a black, noseless cadaver's head stinking of vinegar. How much can a writer take when she wants to change your life, place you dead center where even electroshock can't wipe out the cadaver's head "floating up between my eggs and bacon at breakfast."?

All the June Saturday afternoon Sam Pollit's children
were on the lookout for him as they skated round the dirt
sidewalks and seamed old asphalt of R Street and Reservoir

Road that bounded the deep-grassed acres of Tohoga House, their home. They were not usually allowed to run helter-skelter about the streets, but Sam was out late with the naturalists looking for lizards and salamanders round the Potomac bluffs, Henrietta, their mother, was in town, Bonnie, their youthful aunt and general servant, had her afternoon off, and they were being minded by Louisa, their half sister, eleven and a half years old, the eldest of their brood. Strict and anxious when their parents were at home, Louisa when left in sole command was benevolent, liking to hear their shouts from a distance while she lay on her belly, reading, at the top of the orchard, or ambled, woolgathering, about the house.

The sun dropped between reefs of cloud into the Virginia woods: a rain frog rattled and the air grew damp. Mother coming home from the Wisconsin Avenue car, with parcels, was seen from various corners by the perspiring young ones, who rushed to meet her, chirring on their skates, and who convoyed her home, doing figures round her, weaving and blowing about her or holding to her skirt, and merry, in spite of her decorous irritations.

"I come home and find you tearing about the streets like mad things!"

—*The Man Who Loved Children* (1940), Christina Stead

Of all the books or novels by women in *First Paragraphs*, this is the one I'd most like to have written. I admire the lyricism of Carson McCullers, Marguerite Young, Sylvia Plath, Virginia Woolf, and the others, but Christina Stead—whose paragraphs above have songnotes only in passing, and may even sound flat and characterless to some readers—I envy. Stead's originality drives us down page after page, her ear invents fearlessly, her eye enriches each detail, she brings a houseful of children and adults alive with a heart that reads the finest subtleties as easily as you or I might read a large-type fairy tale. Hers is *the* American family novel, the master-piece no American writer has matched—and she's an Australian.

In *The Man Who Loved Children* Stead uproots her childhood in New South Wales and replants it in a suburb of Washington, D.C., trims it with American talk, energizes it with American hopes and ideals, and shapes it for tragedy. We may or may not sense that the story has been told by the family's eldest child, Louisa, who is set free by the tragedy. At eleven and a half, Louie, or Louisa, knows she's a genius and is always shifting her chores about, hiding from her father, and overseeing her younger half-brothers and half-sister in ways that still allow her to write or read—she even reads in the outdoor shower, the book propped on a crossbeam! She hoards being alone. Her gifts go unsung. She's fat and messy, always dropping, smashing or bending things:

> . . . She was always shamefaced and clumsy . . . She slopped liquids all over the place, stumbled and fell when carrying buckets, could never stand straight to fold the sheets and tablecloths from the wash without giggling or dropping them in the dirt, fell over invisible creases in rugs, was unable to do her hair neatly, and was always leopard-spotted yellow and blue with old and new bruises. She shut drawers on her fingers and doors on her hands, bumped her nose on the wall, and many a time felt like banging her head against the wall in order to reach oblivion and get out of all this strange place in time where she was a square peg in a round hole. (pp. 58–59)

Louie is not alone in these injuries, all the children receive wounds daily: ". . . every such thing left its tiny scar, but their infant skins healed with wonderful quickness."

Not only the children know wounds. Their meanspirited mother Henrietta feels that the whole house is a wound in which she suffers with her detestable brood and hateful husband:

> Henny had never lived in an apartment . . . she belonged to this house and it to her. Though she was a prisoner in it, she possessed it. She and it were her marriage. She was indwelling in every board and stone of it; every fold in the curtains had a meaning (perhaps they were so folded to hide a darn or stain); every room was a phial of revelation to be poured out some feverish night in the secret laboratories of her decisions, full of living cancers of insult, leprosies of disillusion, abscesses of grudge, gangrene of nevermore, quintan fevers of divorce, and all the proliferating miseries, the running sores and thick scabs, for which (and not for its heavenly joys) the flesh of marriage is so heavily veiled and conventually interned.

I love that. The odd words keep with the family's manner of making up a weird, babyish wordbag for itself. Quintan means a fever that gives you the shakes, and conventually interned means that Henny is a nun stuck in a convent—she and Sam sleep apart. It's Sam who has got the family into the strange language he can't help spouting (it lifts his ego and walls him off from unwanted feelings), a language full of politics, science, speeches for mankind, and babytalk. When he's too outrageous, Stead gives us subtitles. A poorly schooled poor boy with a large knowledge of plants and animals, Sam received his job as a naturalist with the Smithsonian Institute through the good graces of his father-in-law, who also rents him the house the family lives in—and Henny hates. He pumps himself full of hot air day and night, foresees greatness for himself, spreads cheer and love over his children as if driven by pitchforks. The reader strangles in his false greatheartedness, the flood of it awes you. At first you can't believe him, Stead seemingly has a tin ear for Sam—then you find she hears only too well. And his blowhard cheer is balanced in the plot by Henny's meanness, self-centered airs and graces and nasty tongue for the world, qualities she well knows she has. One of the book's joys is everyone's self-knowledge, each child a busy little being-in-itself, quite apart from Sam and Henny, as are the lesser characters. The springs of the tragedy are best left for you to find out for yourself—and, please, skip any foreword until you've read the book. Just plunge in.

This book was dangerous to write and killed Stead in the market. Her novel before this, *The House of All Nations* (1938), a blistering, 790-page monster about the money scams of an international banking family, was well-liked and a best-seller. Long as it was, it did not set up bookbuyers for the tragic upheavals of *The Man Who Loved Children* (1940), whose 527 pages Stead wrote in her late thirties at the height of her intellectual and physical vigor—and with the knowledge that she had already unraveled the vast entanglements of international finance. What problems could a little family novel hold? Well, quite a few! She states and restates that children have "no rights"—and in the Pollit family get strangled, beaten and eaten alive daily, as their crawly father endlessly sucks love from their throats; no rights in the horrifying, but funny, fishbowl in which they drown while snapping at each other. Stead's complete absence of hearts and flowers, her naked eye taking it all in, both at a remove and then in the minds of the pricked children, the mean mother, the raving father, are all shown with wit, the sure poetic phrase, and the breathlessly perfect line of dialogue. All this moves toward a blowout meant to send the reader skidding over a cliff. That was the year my mother took *Ladies Home Journal, Good Housekeeping, Cosmopolitan* and *Woman's Home Companion*, and the big names strewn around our house were Daphne Du Maurier, Vicki Baum, Pearl Buck and Fannie Hurst. Meanwhile in *The New Yorker*, Clifton Fadiman was saying about this novel, "The book is *Little Women* rewritten by a demon . . . as a whole [it] does not come off," while in *The New Republic* Mary McCarthy said:

> This is not the first time the unconscious hypocrite has been stripped naked. What is "original" and "extraordinary" in Miss Stead's treatment is the fearful, disordered vindictiveness with which she pursues her character . . . At first the reader is seriously shocked and repelled; then he is moved to doubt and hot denial, and finally, like the Pollit children again, he becomes indifferent, and the author is obliged to pile up a whole heap of Gothic horrors at the end to attract his numbed attention.
>
> —Mary McCarthy, *The New Republic* (January 13, 1941)

The novel sank and was not seen again for twenty-eight years, when it arose in paperback reprint and has since been more or less at hand, should you have heard about it. Stead never again wrote as ambitious a novel as *The Man Who Loved Children*. Her scope narrowed. Though she wrote several more novels, she was seldom spoken of in America as any kind of literary force.

Not long after her 1941 review of *The Man Who Loved Children*, Mary McCarthy published her own first novel, which begins:

> She could not bear to hurt her husband. She impressed this on the Young Man, on her confidantes, and finally on her husband himself. The thought of Telling Him actually made her heart turn over in a sudden and sickening way, she said. This was true, and yet she knew that being a potential divorcee was deeply pleasurable in somewhat the same way that being an engaged girl had been. In both cases, there was at first a subterranean courtship, whose significance it was necessary to conceal from outside

observers. The concealment of the original, premarital courtship had, however, been a mere superstitious gesture, briefly sustained. It had also been, on the whole, a private secretiveness, not a partnership of silence. One put one's family and one's friends off the track because one was still afraid that the affair might not come out right, might not lead in a clean, direct line to the altar. To confess one's aspirations might be, in the end, to publicize one's failure. Once a solid understanding had been reached, there followed a short intermission of ritual bashfulness, in which both parties awkwardly participated, and then came the Announcement.

—*The Company She Keeps* (1943), Mary McCarthy

This is smart, amusing and not to be knocked. It might even be worthwhile to have your child skewered by a wit like Mc-Carthy's, especially when she is Mrs. Edmund Wilson, wife of the nation's leading literary critic. She just *might* want to knock out a novelist upstream of her who is already being called, without McCarthy's loaded quotes, "original" and "extraordinary"—and who also has had a huge, well-received and marvelously well-written bestseller in *House of All Nations*, a work far beyond McCarthy's clever powers. But it's fifty years later, why bring this up? Just to show: writing is dangerous, even for geniuses.

As I say, McCarthy's drollery is not to be knocked. But 223 pages of waggishness is more than I'd care to stand up for.

It was an extraordinary night.

The wind had been blowing; it had ceased, and the stars had sprouted like weeds. They were in tufts with roots of gold, full-blown, sunk into the darkness and raising shining masses of night.

Jourdan could not sleep. He turned and tossed.

"The night is wonderfully bright," he said to himself.

He had never seen the like before.

The sky was vibrating like a sheet of metal. You could not tell what made it do so because all was still, even the tiniest willow twig. It was not the wind. It was simply that the sky came down and touched the earth, raked the plains, struck the mountains, and made the corridors of the forests ring. Then it rose once more to the far heights.

—*Joy of Man's Desiring*, Jean Giono (1935; translated by Katherine Allen Clarke)

Giono divorces himself from the social and political life of France between the great wars and listens for the song of Pan massing the night with stars, flooding man with sunrise and his nerves with urges, threading the earth with roots and bursting the skins of seedlings, blowing in the cold morning spumes of beasts. Nobody anywhere writes from the Pan-spirit quite as Giono does among the peasants of the French countryside, although, in his poems, D. H. Lawrence knows Pan just as livingly, as does Knut Hamsun in his novels, *Pan*, *Mysteries* and *Growth of the Soil* (at times my favorite twentieth-century novel). But the problems of Hamsun's and Lawrence's characters are far from those of Giono's.

This is the story of a Pan-spirited acrobat who falls among the rock-bottom peasant farmers of Southern France. Settling down, he spreads his spirit among them. The peasants turn from their old ways, their hunting and crop-raising, and invest themselves into making an Earthly Paradise full of love and flowers. The joy of man's desiring comes to be—but tragedy strikes.

This passionate opening shows Giono's style at its most burnished and grand, perhaps even Biblical. Fervor sweeps through everything that follows, and when his haunting effects take hold, you jump in your chair: Ready for a fearless cosmic renewal, to hunker down with fox and lizard, have your face oiled with the rain, your fingers sticky with the blood of kids and skinned hares as you roast the creatures:

. . . he pointed to the granite heart of the storm that was falling straight down from the heights of the sky, and suddenly they were all lashed by stiff rain and the wind pushed against their backs, raised the dust, bore off the hot embers on its wings, made the larding pin sing as it trembled beneath the weight of the kid. The thick odor of damp earth. (p. 138)

Better than nature movies on TV? You bet. But Giono faced his dangers, too. Who could believe in all this Pan stuff in 1935 with economies in depression and Hitler on the march? Should Giono write it or shouldn't he? He went with his blood and wrote it. A novel, after all, is not only a strategy of words, it's also a long and cunning arrangement of feelings you desire to pass on, and Hitler did not stir any feelings Giono wanted to give his current or future readers. A silly choice, to turn a blind eye to economics and a raging dictator? Well, his book's still here and the Third Reich isn't.

What made me take this trip to Africa? There is no quick explanation. Things got worse and worse and worse and pretty soon they were too complicated.

When I think of my condition at the age of fifty-five when I bought the ticket, all is grief. The facts begin to crowd me and soon I get a pressure in the chest. A disorderly rush begins—my parents, my wives, my children, my farm, my animals, my habits, my money, my music lessons, my drunkenness, my prejudices, my brutality, my teeth, my face, my soul! I have to cry, "No, no, get back, curse you, let me alone!" But how can they let me alone? They belong to me. They are mine. And they pile into me from all sides. It turns into chaos.

—*Henderson the Rain King* (1959), Saul Bellow

This is my favorite Bellow novel and favorite first paragraph by him. For once he is not bending every phrase to a rococo turn. Many readers may favor his richer style, but I find I get bogged down. For example, I read four-fifths of *Humboldt's Gift* (1976) and quit. There was not going to be a payoff and I'd lost interest in fine writing. There had not been a payoff in *Mr. Sammler's Planet* (1970) or in *Herzog* (1964), though I'd finished them and thought them marvelously written. Even *Henderson* has, for me, a pasteboard payoff: I just don't believe in the hero's change of character. But *Henderson* kept me gripped. I often have much the same problem with E. L. Doctorow, whose fine writing at last swamps all story interest for me. This is in part because Doctorow—aside from being a great artist and, in person, a human being as attractive as any living man—is a social historian who writes novels, and, for him, density of expressive detail is quite as ravishing as the storytelling. I'm thinking of *Billy Bathgate*—I read three-fourths of it and quit. It was not going to rise above its fine writing, and I did not have to stay around to prove it to myself. For me, Bellow and Doctorow share this shortcoming, of firing elephant guns at lions.

Here is the opening of Bellow's novel which came just before *Henderson* and from which the style of *Henderson* pulls back:

> I am an American, Chicago born—Chicago, that somber city—and go at things as I have taught myself, free-style, and will make the record in my own way: first to knock, first admitted, sometimes an innocent knock, sometimes a not so innocent. But a man's character is his fate, says Heraclitus, and in the end there isn't any way to disguise the nature of the knocks by accoustical work on the door or gloving the knuckles.
> —*The Adventures of Augie March* (1953), Saul Bellow

Many may like this more than the freer line of *Henderson*, but, for me, it's overcooked. You have to stop and go through the changes with Bellow of how he got to "gloving the knuckles" from "with gloves on" and what he means by "there isn't any way to disguise the nature of the knocks by accoustical work on the door. . . ." From whom would he disguise the knocks? From fate?—are these the opening knocks of Beethoven's *Fifth*? Have we leaped from Heraclitus to Beethoven? What does accoustical work on the door mean? Softening the blows of fate? But Augie is doing the knocking, not fate. Does Chicago being somber have something to do with this? Could first to knock, first admitted be a proverb I've not heard before?

Now, I have no question at all that Bellow knows exactly what he means and could clear this up for me in thirty seconds. But all I have is me, and I dislike having to straighten out the loopings of this drawn out knocking simile; I feel disheartened when a first paragraph stops me flat and I can't make sense of it. For me, Augie's going at things free-style and making the record in his own way has nothing to do with first to knock, first admitted, whether it's an innocent knock, not so innocent, gloved, or disguised by corkboard. And this is what in Bellow sometimes delights but often overwhelms me: he's LETTING ME KNOW that he's writing. But—is this knocking Bellow's, or Augie's, hollow simile? Is Bellow having a joke on Augie, giving him a lofty style that shows us he's hollow? Hard to say, since the fine workmanship of gloving the knuckles strives for excellence and fails only as writing for angels. This opening even resists the dreaded Dr. Don rewrite, which we tried out on *Rabbit at Rest*, since I don't know what the paragraph's about. So I give up. Do *Understanding Poetry* and *The Reader Over Your Shoulder* blind me with hairsplitting? Not with Bellow. He splits his own hairs, subatomically—but at a level of physics I can't follow.

No such trouble in *Henderson*. Here Bellow writes under full steam, at the crest of his vigor in his early forties, and in his first paragraphs is the Promethean satirist unbound by simile. This novel begins in today's world with larger-than-life Eugene Henderson, a millionaire swamped by his own hungers and marriages and off-spring. We laugh at his pains and, in the spirit of Bellow's satirical realism, take them as our own. Then Henderson goes to Africa, the close household satire broadens into a huge fantasy of an Africa of the mind, and Henderson comes to grips with his hungers while embroiled with the first gods of man's beginnings. Out of his perils in this crucible, he chooses to become a doctor, then flies home to go to medical school and help mankind.

Something about the ending fails; perhaps I've failed to follow the story closely enough. But I think not, since Bellow's longer novels always drown the story in wit and detail. For me, the pre-African pages are the high point in all Bellow, his great humor at perfect pitch. I'm quite sorry when Gene goes to Africa and gets tested by a nearly book-length fantasy. I want him tested at home, not in Never-never Land. But it's the storyteller's right, in fact, his need and hunger, much like Henderson's, to do what his imagination tells him, and so I follow Henderson along into his new life behind the mask of tribal rain king. Somehow, all that doesn't tie in with my deepest needs, how to harness my own wild horses *without* going to Africa. I could say that this is a Jungian Africa, where I'm meeting archetypal figures from my own unconscious, but that would be to deny Bellow his whole intent, to plunge me into a totally unfamiliar place where logic is winged magic and I learn by being bared to ideas and dangers from the first boilings of man's mind, not from books. If that's what the novel's about; I could be all wet. Anyway, if I'm willing, and time and again I am, to follow Mahler's ten symphonies through the wildest emotional country, and have come to enjoy even his marches and burlesques of musical forms I was never familiar with in the first place, why can't I march with Bellow into Africa and trust him to bring me through as fulfillingly as Mahler does? Is this apples and oranges? Well, in *Henderson* I am willing. When the brawling, paunchy, six-foot-four, middleaged, married, violin-playing pig-farmer, Gene Henderson, first goes to seduce young Lily in her hopeless tenement on Hudson Street and climbs the staircase to her door, telling us, "I came, a great weight, a huge shadow on those stairs, with my face full of country color and booze, and yellow pigskin gloves on my hands, and a ceaseless voice in my heart that said, *I want, I want, I want, oh, I want—yes, go on,* I said to myself, *Strike, strike, strike, strike!* And I kept going on the staircase in my thick padded coat, in pigskin gloves and pigskin shoes, a pigskin wallet in my pocket, seething with lust and seething with trouble, and realizing how my gaze glittered up to the top bannister where Lily had opened the door and was waiting," I am well and truly hooked for the distance. I'll go anywhere with this writer. Later, while fighting with Lily, whom he's married, he rises from the breakfast table and goes to see why the housekeeper hasn't brought their eggs:

> I went into the kitchen and saw this old creature lying dead on the floor. During my rage, her heart had stopped. The eggs were still boiling; they bumped the sides of the pot as eggs will do when the water is seething. I turned off the gas. Dead! Her small, toothless face, to which I laid my knuckles, was growing cold. The soul, like a current of air, like a draft, like a bubble, sucked out of the window. I stared at her. So this is it, the end—farewell? And all this while, these days and weeks, the wintry garden had been speaking to me of this fact and no other; and till this moment I had not understood what this gray and white and brown, the bark, the snow, the twigs, had been telling me. I said nothing to Lily. Not knowing what else to do, I wrote a note DO NOT DISTURB and pinned it to the old lady's skirt, and I went through the frozen winter garden and across the road to her garden. (p. 36)

Here's heaven. I feel heartbreak. Here is the high song *Augie* seeks—facts, facts, feelingful facts—and no amount of fine striving with phrases can make *Augie* sing. It's will power against heart power, a brass band unable to float like a violin.

The reviews ran heavily against *Henderson*. Sales were disappointing. Bellow always tries to open up when he writes, but this time he'd given up many of his tricks and tried for a kind straightforward factuality that would be fun to watch. That's why the opening works so well. "What made me take this trip to Africa?" Henderson asks. All the complications, the grief—and then he swells with *the facts* (not a simile knocking on a door)—"my parents, my wives, my girls, my children, my farm, my animals, my habits, my money, my music lessons, my drunkenness, my prejudices, my brutality, my teeth, my face, my soul!" Chaos. Lovely chaos, eyed fact by fact.

That's the danger, when you strip yourself down and go for the facts. The tastemakers, used to your old silverpoint phrases and fussy about facing a new you when the old one's nicely catalogued, will turn and run long needles through your heart and your eyes and your book—and they did. *Henderson*'s an odd, funny, bravura show, in which Bellow sets out to work without his usual verbal net, and in the long run his nervy liveliness, forward-moving story, and agonized but always dancing hero may well fare better than his whole team of learned heroes.

In 1979, when asked about *Henderson the Rain King*'s low sales and bad showing with the reviewers, Bellow said, "Oh, well, I just write stories." He said also that *Henderson* was his favorite novel among his works.

But he never wrote that clearly at that length again.

In 1902 Father built a house at the crest of the Broadview Avenue hill in New Rochelle, New York. It was a three-story shingle with dormers, bay windows and a screened porch. Striped awnings shaded the windows. The family took possession of this stout manse on a sunny day in June and it seemed for some years thereafter that all their days would be warm and fair. The best part of Father's income was derived from the manufacture of flags and buntings and other accoutrements of patriotism, including fireworks. Patriotism was a reliable sentiment in the early 1900's.

Teddy Roosevelt was President. The population customarily gathered in great numbers either out of doors for parades, public concerts, fish fries, political picnics, social outings, or indoors in meeting halls, vaudeville theatres, operas, ballrooms. There seemed to be no entertainment that did not involve great swarms of people. Trains and steamers and trolleys moved them from one place to another. That was the style, that was the way people lived. Women were stouter then. They visited the fleet carrying white parasols. Everyone wore white in summer. Tennis racquets were hefty and the racquet faces elliptical. There was a lot of sexual fainting. There were no Negroes. There were no immigrants. On Sunday afternoon, after dinner, Father and Mother went upstairs and closed the bedroom door. Grandfather fell asleep on the divan in the parlor. The Little Boy in the sailor blouse sat on the screened porch and waved away the flies. Down at the bottom of the hill Mother's Younger Brother boarded the streetcar and rode to the end of the line. He was a lonely, withdrawn young man with blond moustaches, and was thought to be having difficulty finding himself. The end of the line was an empty field of tall marsh grasses. The air was salt. Mother's Younger Brother in his white linen suit and boater rolled his trousers and walked barefoot in the salt marshes. Sea birds started and flew up. This was the time in our history when Winslow Homer was doing his painting. A certain light was still available along the Eastern seaboard. Homer painted the light. It gave the sea a heavy dull menace and shone coldly on the rocks and shoals of the New England coast. There were unexplained shipwrecks and brave towline rescues. Odd things went on in lighthouses and in shacks nestled in the wild beach plum. Across America sex and death were barely distinguishable. Runaway women died in the rigors of ecstasy. Stories were hushed up and reporters paid off by rich families. One read between the lines of the journals and gazettes. In New York City the papers were full of the shooting of the famous architect Stanford White by Harry K. Thaw, eccentric scion of a coke and railroad fortune. Harry K. Thaw was the husband of Evelyn Nesbit, the celebrated beauty who had once been Stanford White's mistress. The shooting took place in the roof garden of the Madison Square Garden on 26th Street, a spectacular block-long building of yellow brick and terra cotta that White himself had designed in the Sevillian style. It was the opening night of a revue entitled *Mamzelle Champagne*, and as the chorus sang and danced the eccentric scion wearing on this summer night a straw boater and heavy black coat pulled out a pistol and shot the famous architect three times in the head. On the roof. There were screams. Evelyn fainted. She had been a well-known artist's model at the age of fifteen. Her underclothes were white. Her husband habitually whipped her. She happened once to meet Emma Goldman, the revolutionary. Goldman lashed her with her tongue. Apparently there *were* Negroes. There *were* immigrants. And though the newspaper called the shooting the Crime of the Century, Goldman knew it was only 1906 and there were ninety-four years to go.

—*Ragtime* (1974), E. L. Doctorow

This rapturous paragraph, about fabled times, is five paragraphs brilliantly run together that speak of five of the novel's larger themes. The natural breaks fall after "all their days would be warm and fair;" "that was the way people lived;" "There were no immigrants;" "Seabirds started and flew up;" and "nestled in the wild beach plum."

Two qualities strike you right off. The declaring of each sentence and the lay of light on the sentence. God might even be saying, Let there be light on America, except that neither God nor church is spoken of anywhere. So perhaps it is some gifted social historian, since his voice tries less to interest us in events rather than in cultural detail. Not that there aren't interesting events, a wandering young man with an unformed sense of self, a murder, a famous tabloid emptyhead meeting a famous revolutionary, with delicious subevents about Father and Mother having sex on Sunday, and Evelyn's white underclothes—we wonder, did they show when she fainted? Seemingly a tossed off detail, they return as part of the novel's design when Mother's Younger Brother, hiding in a closet, watches Evelyn undress. The white underclothes, in fact, become a rhapsody of imprisonment as Doctorow unveils layer after layer of Evelyn's corseting and understraps.

The mix of cultural detail and story remains at this level throughout the novel. We see no thing without its placement among other things and events. As the novel moves along, it gains a symphonic effect, a sound much larger than ragtime, though the muted gaiety and melancholy of a Scott Joplin rag is never far off. We might think of all this detail as skipping or cascading piano notes, with heavier chords sometime springing or darkening the rhythm. I don't think Doctorow built his novel as strongly on likenesses to music as many reviewers read into it, or if he did, it comes through only to the eye, not the heart.

Doctorow stands back from each sentence, never sweetens it, or makes it sour. He's rarely involved with feelings. We infer them from what happens, although a sense of homecoming hangs everywhere as the reader discovers his own lost past, a past awakening on familial brain cells bearing sounds and scenery from before his birth. But even this is not pushed at us, every detail is given baldly, and we must enter it or not as we will: "The walls were a faded lilac print. An electric lamp at the bedside provided the only light." *Were* is passive and *provided* is neutral, you may experience the scene at any intensity you desire, this grandmaster of set design does not force on you his lilac wall and bedlamp. The past arises gently, in a breath, a gesture, a ribbon. If a feeling were underlined, the novel's purposeful march would falter. As it is, the title sheds feeling on every page, keeps us fresh with delight as themes weave together. My favorite scene is Chapter Twenty, when billionaire J. P. Morgan tries to bring assembly line genius Henry Ford into a secret ring of men of great wealth, breathing together to shape a new world order. But even this is told to us at a slight remove, we are not being sold Morgan's ideas about himself and Ford embodying a secret wisdom, a magic that ensures their return in coming ages when they will go on bringing light and health to mankind. Only later do we sense Doctorow's spellbound smile, like Cheshire Cat's, hanging in the air over Morgan and Ford.

Written as he turned forty, *The Book of Daniel* (1972) is Doctorow's strongest, largest, and most intense novel, but I'll never read it again. *Ragtime*, coasting off of the powers of *Daniel*, is his most entertaining, and one I never pick up without feeling rewarded. It will likely remain as his masterpiece.

During these last decades the interest in professional fasting has markedly diminished. It used to pay very well to stage such great performances under one's own management, but today that is quite impossible. We live in a different world now. At one time the whole town took a lively interest in the hunger artist; from day to day of his fast the excitement mounted; everybody wanted to see him at least once a day; there were people who bought season tickets for the last few days and sat from morning till night in front of his small barred cage; even in the nighttime there were visiting hours, when the whole effect was heightened by torch flares; on fine days the cage was set out in the open air, and then it was the children's special treat to see the hunger artist; for their elders he was often just a joke that happened to be in fashion, but the children stood openmouthed, holding each other's hands for greater security, marveling at him as he sat there pallid in black tights, with his ribs sticking out so prominently, not even on a seat but down among straw on the ground, sometimes giving a courteous nod, answering questions with a constrained smile, or perhaps stretching an arm through the bars so that one might feel how thin it was, and then again withdrawing deep into himself, paying no attention to anyone or anything, not even to the all-important striking of the clock that was the only piece of furniture in his cage, but merely staring into vacancy with half-shut eyes, now and then taking a sip from a tiny glass of water to moisten his lips.

> —"The Hunger Artist" (1922), *The Complete Stories* (1978), Franz Kafka

The structure of this great opening tells us a lot about the voice. It opens with three simple sentences, then falls into an endlessness we now think of as European. Nobody builds sentences like that anymore and gets published—not in America. The big sentence starts as a series of plain statements with semicolons for rest stops, statements simple enough for a child to take in; and then it falls into an easy-flowing rich braid of clauses that slowly suck you in and bring you to the last image, "a sip from a tiny glass of water to moisten his lips."

What is the voice? At first it's historical. The baldness of it slides right over the landmine phrase "professional fasting"—the germ of the story—almost as if this storyteller had said, The interest in professional suicide has markedly diminished. What can that mean, professional fasting? He's not going to tell us in the next two sentences. Our curiosity grows, as he sighs, We live in a different world now, as if professional fasting were once as common as the neglected sport of pitching horseshoes. Then he bores in, the historical voice fading as he speaks of the hunger artist. Who's this bizarre person? And the voice lifts; gets tenory, as if speaking to children, oh, the excitement. Everybody wanted to see him at least once a day! Good heavens, we bought season tickets for the last few days and sat FROM MORNING TILL NIGHT in front of his *small—barred—cage*. . . . Even in the nighttime—oh, you should have seen it—there were visiting hours, and the whole effect was heightened—listen—by torch flares—can you believe it—we all sat around there at night watching. Now, on fine days *the cage* was set out in the open air—and that was a special treat, the kids loved it, to see the hunger artist. Okay, for the elders he was just a joke, a fad—but the *children* stood there openmouthed. Openmouthed—holding each other's hands, they were shaken! They marveled at him. He sat there, so pale in black tights, ugh! His ribs sticking out *in ridges*. No stool, he sat in the straw on the ground, you could get right up to him, three feet. But he was courteous, he'd nod, try to smile answering your questions. And, *oh*, he'd put his arm out through the bars . . . you could *feel* how thin it was, whooh! And then he'd withdraw, into himself, the arm you'd touched, and pay no attention to anyone. He couldn't even hear the very important clock in his cage when it struck (it was his only piece of furniture, no cup, no table). He'd just stare into the distance with half-shut eyes. And then take—a sip, just a sip—I have to whisper—from a teensy glass of water—to wet, I mean just to *moi isten*—his lips. Aghh, you should have been there . . .

I'm not out to improve Kafka, only to wash out our reading ears. We are so used to the dull voice of silent reading that we can't hear what we read. Great writing TALKS to us. It breathes. It's not engraved on silver. As soon as you can't hear someone speaking to you in a sentence, the writer is writing WRITING and forget it. He's DEAF, he's in love with himself, he's in love with WORDS ON PAPER, not WORDS IN THE EAR.

Shakespeare had the idea.

Polonius: What do you read, my lord?
Hamlet: Words, words, words.

But when Wild Bill wants to shake the wordtree, and encrust the passage with the richest words he can pack together, it's still words for the tongue and the ear:

Hamlet: . . . I have of late—but wherefore I know not—lost
all my mirth, forgone all custom of exercises; and
indeed it goes so heavily with my disposition, that
this goodly frame the earth seems to me a sterile
promontory, this most excellent canopy the air, look
you, this brave o'er-hanging firmament, this majesti-
cal roof fretted with golden fire, why it appeareth
nothing to me but a foul and pestilent congregation
of vapors. What a piece of work is a man, how noble
in reason, how infinite in faculties, in form and
moving, how express and admirable in action, how
like an angel in apprehension, how like a god: the
beauty of the world, the paragon of animals. And
yet to me, what is this quintessence of dust? Man
delights me not, nor woman neither, though by your
smiling you seem to say so.
                    —*Hamlet* (1604), William Shakespeare, II.ii

Now how can you write prose more rich than that? And yet,
it's for your ear. 'Nuff said.

I don't have to sell you the Kafka story above. If that
paragraph doesn't send you into "The Hunger Artist" you
shouldn't be reading this book. But read with your EARS.

The thousand injuries of Fortunato I had borne as best
I could; but when he ventured upon insult, I vowed revenge . . .
                    —"A Cask of Amontillado" (1846), Edgar Allan Poe

Poe, writing with his ears. How else would a poet write?

Lolita, light of my life, fire of my loins. My sin, my soul.
Lo-lee-ta: the tip of the tongue taking a trip of three steps
down the palate to tap, at three, on the teeth. Lo. Lee. Ta.
She was Lo, plain Lo, in the morning, standing four feet

ten in one sock. She was Lola in slacks. She was Dolly at school. She was Dolores on the dotted line. But in my arms she was always Lolita.

Did she have a precursor? She did, indeed she did. In point of fact, there might have been no Lolita at all had I not loved, one summer, a certain initial girl-child. In a princedom by the sea. Oh when? About as many years before Lolita was born as my age was that summer. You can always count on a murderer for a fancy prose style.

Ladies and gentlemen of the jury, exhibit number one is what the seraphs, the misinformed, simple, noble-winged seraphs, envied. Look at this tangle of thorns.

—*Lolita* (1956), Vladimir Nabokov

My God, what can I say about this? Absolutely nothing. I quote it because Look at this tangle of thorns leaves me swimming in bliss.

Nabokov is surely the fanciest stylist of the century, at least in English. No one but Joyce weighs words more finely. His voice never fails him. You may not like *what* he says, but he says it exactly and always with a Nabokovian air. He has recorded the outrageous scene of the shooting of Quilty and reads it from Olympus (". . . I went about lucidly insane, crazily calm . . ."), a scene whose parody of T. S. Eliot's "Ash Wednesday" I'd always thought failed on the page. But once you hear the master read that scene, whoo!—it's alive and Quilty snivels gloriously. I had wax in my ears when I first read it in 1956, a wax put there by the reviewers who adored Nabokov's Fine Prose Style, and so I read with the deafness known only by those obsessed with Fine Prose. The voice escaped me. Even the voice of the first paragraphs above. I read *She was Lo, plain Lo, in the morning, standing four feet ten in one sock* with a merciless eye, because in those days I could only read with my eyes.

As you read this, try to hear a Spanish accent, a bit flowery, one hand perhaps spelling things in the air:

Many years later, as he faced the firing squad, Colonel Aureliano Buendia was to remember that distant afternoon when his father took him to discover ice. At that time Macondo was a village of twenty adobe houses, built on the bank of a river of clear water that ran along a bed of polished stones, which were white and enormous, like prehistoric eggs. The world was so recent that many things lacked names, and in order to indicate them it was necessary to point. Every year during the month of March a family of ragged gypsies would set up their tents near the village, and with a great uproar of pipes and kettledrums they would display new inventions. First they brought the magnet. A heavy gypsy with an untamed beard and sparrow hands, who introduced himself as Melquiades, put on a bold public demonstration of what he himself called the eighth wonder of the learned alchemists of Macedonia. He went from house to house dragging two metal ingots and everybody was amazed to see pots, pans, tongs, and braziers tumble down from their places and beams creak from the desperation of nails and screws trying to emerge, and even objects that had been lost for a long time appeared from where they had been searched for most and went dragging along in turbulent confusion behind Melquiades' magical irons. "Things have a life of their own," the gypsy proclaimed with a harsh accent. "It's simply a matter of waking up their souls." Jose Arcadio Buendia, whose unbridled imagination always went beyond the genius of nature and even beyond miracles and magic, thought that it would be possible to make use of that useless invention to extract gold from the bowels of the earth. Melquiades, who was an honest man, warned him: "It won't work for that." But Jose Arcadio Buendia at that time did not believe in the honesty of gypsies, so he traded his mule and a pair of goats for the two magnetized ingots. Ursula Iguaran, his wife, who relied on those animals to increase their poor domestic holdings, was unable to dissuade him. "Very soon we'll have gold enough and more to pave the floors of the house," her husband replied. For several months he worked hard to demonstrate the truth of his idea. He explored every inch of the region, even the riverbed, dragging the two iron ingots along and reciting Melquiades' incantation aloud. The only thing he succeeded in doing was to unearth a suit of fifteenth-century armor which had all of its pieces soldered together with rust and inside of which there was the hollow resonance of an enormous stone-filled gourd. When Jose Arcadio Buendia and the four men of his expedition managed to take the armor apart, they found inside a calcified skeleton with a copper locket containing a woman's hair around its neck.

> —*One Hundred Years of Solitude* (1967), Gabriel Garcia Marquez (Englished by Gregory Rabassa)

Before I go on, I think the last sentence in this otherwise entrancing retonguing from the Spanish should read "they found inside a calcified skeleton and around its neck a copper locket containing a woman's hair." I doubt that the original says "a copper locket containing a woman's hair around its neck."

This big paragraph sounds many themes that follow. Perhaps the largest theme we meet is the split between facts and magic, although the sense of the earth's just being born is quite strong. The book's method throughout intends to balance each paragraph with facts and magic, and create in us a hunger for its author's imagination and the voice of magic realism. His facts bind us to earth, his magic lets us soar. When this novel first came out in English, in 1970, most readers were enchanted by what seemed a new find in Spanish fiction: magic realism. Its appeal, the release it offered readers and wild freedom for writers, was like waking from muddy dreams to clear daylight. Writers were suddenly granted magic, if they could just bend it to their own use. Of course, Don Quixote fighting the windmills which he thinks are giants differs little from Jose Arcadia Buendia dragging magnets through riverbeds in search of gold nuggets. The Tolstoy tale about Esarhaddon uses magic realism so naturally—with Esarhaddon turning into King Lailie and then into a she-ass—that the reader feels a starburst when each magic event takes place; storytelling is no longer earthbound; but Tolstoy is not interested in using magic to pour out songlike words. The fearless mastery of his magic turns on moral hardness; it's not there to sweeten or seduce us.

Garcia Marquez drops us into the small abandoned village of Macondo in a nameless South American country. We live in it for a hundred years, off in the jungle, beyond railroad or light bulb. In the world outside, invention is seething and changing the nature of civilization. In Macondo, the leading inventor is Jose Arcadio Buendia, "whose unbridled imagination always went beyond the genius of nature and even beyond miracles and magic," and he is full of illusions. One of the great moments of the novel—in fact, one of the great moments in modern writing—is at the end of the first chapter, when the gypsies open a trunk and show him a great block of ice, something he has never seen before and at first thinks is the largest diamond in the world, and then, for a total of thirty-five *reales*, allow him to lay hand on its fearful mystery. Delirious with this "prodigious experience," he pays "and with hand on the cake, as if giving testimony on the holy scriptures, he exclaimed: 'This is the great invention of our time'."

We follow the rise of Macondo and the Buendia family, the coming of violence, selfish profit, slow death, disillusion, inbreeding, and the birth in the seventh generation of Buendias of a pig-tailed boy, who heralds the cataclysmic cyclone that tears Macondo to bits and returns it to the waiting jungle. The rising action of the novel, its comic spirit, breathless storytelling, heavenly flowerfall of magic, and the growth of Macondo and the Buendias, lift us with delight. But when the tragic fall begins, its endless dark notes dim our eagerness to read on. We do, and the author is still playful and talking to us with his hat tilted sidewise, but, for me, the darkness and decline strike me as a lesser fulfilling of the novel's lifespirit than Garcia Marquez might have found while keeping to the truth of his vision. The ending is vivid, never less than inspired in each detail, the story rounding itself out with marvels. Perhaps the possibilities in magic realism itself fall short of the notes I want to ring off the anvil.

There was once a priest with cold, watery eyes, who, in the still of the night, wept cold tears. He wept because the afternoons were warm and long, and he was unable to attain a complete mystical union with our Lord. Sometimes, near four o'clock, there was a rustle of Swede girls along the path by his window, and in their shrill laughter he found a terrible dissonance that made him pray aloud for the twilight to come. At twilight the laughter and the voices were quieter, but several times he had walked past Romberg's Drug Store when it was dusk and the yellow lights shone inside and the nickel taps of the soda-fountain were gleaming, and he had found the scent of cheap toilet soap desperately sweet upon the air. He passed that way when he returned from hearing confessions on Saturday nights, and he grew careful to walk on the other side of the street so that the smell of the soap would float upward before it reached his nostrils as it drifted, rather like incense, toward the summer moon.

—"Absolution" *(1924), The Short Stories of F. Scott Fitzgerald (1989)*

Any story that starts this lyrically has to get down to earth soon, and Fitzgerald's does. It's about a priest who has no place to hide from God and an eleven-year-old adolescent German Catholic boy, with a strictly religious father, who finds himself parting from God, to save himself. At first, young Rudolph Miller walks about creating an alter ego, Blatchford Sarnemington. He has no idea that this is his way of defending his ego at a deeper level. Rudolph has not been to confession for over a month when, in the confessional itself, he commits a sin by lying to a priest, then is so haunted by it that he cannot face God in communion. So he makes a separate peace with God, whom he believes in, and keeps a little corner of himself safe from God's walking in on him. Even so, his agony drives him one day to see the cold-weeping priest of the first paragraph and confess his half-buried lie in the confessional. But while he's talking, his agony carries the repressed priest over the brink, and the priest falls into bizarre speeches. Natural impulses springing from the rustle of Swedish girls along the path by his window, or from the fertility of the wheat waving under "the unavoidable sun," have driven the priest so firmly beyond absolution—and perhaps, he may fear, into apostasy—that he goes mad. He weeps, we are told in the first two sentences, because he is "unable to attain a complete mystical union with our Lord." He's far gone, and in a longer story we'd know more about the hunger that impels him to complete mystical union. As it is, we find out more about Rudolph.

After a songlike opening with its strong sexual touches—the priest's mystical longings, rich as incense overcome by perfumes from cheap toilet soap, and the yellow lights and gleaming nickel taps in Romberg's Drug Store that attract us and signal youthful flirting—maybe even petting—the story flows with great naturalness and skill. Fitzgerald may not know quite where he's going with this oddball priest (the seed of whose illness is revealed to us indirectly in Rudolph's father, a religious tyrant), but the story's parts, and the priest, and Rudolph come together at the end with unusual cunning, and we are treated to a wrap-up that repeats the songlike opening. A story about the sexual pathology of a priest in a German and Swedish community was unlikely magazine material in 1924, and quite daring to write, but H. L. Mencken, a wickedly anti-Puritan intellectual of German background, must have lighted a cigar and ordered a fresh draft beer when he bought this one for his new magazine *The American Mercury*. This story, by the way, was written as the prologue to *The Great Gatsby*, in a lost early draft of that novel, then cut when—Fitzgerald said—"it interfered with the neatness of the plan." A wise cut!

Begin with an individual, and before you know it you find that you have created a type; begin with a type, and you find that you have created—nothing. That is because we are all queer fish, queerer behind our faces and voices than we want any one to know or than we know ourselves. When I hear a man proclaiming himself an "average, honest, open fellow," I feel pretty sure that he has some definite and perhaps terrible abnormality which he has agreed to conceal—and his protestation of being average and honest and open is his way of reminding himself of his misprision.

There are no types, no plurals. There is a rich boy, and this is his and not his brothers' story. All my life I have lived among his brothers but this one has been my friend. Besides, if I wrote about his brothers I should have to begin by attacking all the lies that the poor have told about the rich and the rich have told about themselves—such a wild structure they have erected that when we pick up a book about the rich, some instinct prepares us for unreality. Even the intelligent and impassioned reporters of life have made the country of the rich as unreal as fairy-land.

Let me tell you about the very rich. They are different from you and me. They possess and enjoy early, and it does something to them, makes them soft where we are hard, and cynical where we are trustful, in a way that, unless you were born rich, it is very difficult to understand. They think, deep in their hearts, that they are better than we are because we had to discover the compensations and refuges of life for ourselves. Even when they enter deep into our world or sink below us, they still think that they are better than we are. They are different. The only way I can describe young Anson Hunter is to approach him as if he were a foreigner and cling stubbornly to my point of view. If I accept his for a moment I am lost—I have nothing to show but a preposterous movie.

—"The Rich Boy" (1926), *The Short Stories of F. Scott Fitzgerald* (1989)

The only word I'd change in this is "wrongful acts" for "misprision." Misprision is a word nobody remembers the meaning of, unless he's a lawyer, and "his protestation of being average and honest and open is his way of reminding himself of his wrongful acts" for me is stronger—and doesn't stop the story for a run to the dictionary. Also, I'm left hanging by "the compensations and refuges of life" which everyday folks have to find for themselves that the rich are granted at birth. This means fine houses, fine clothes, great food? You and I can have a clean house, a good suit, and a bowl of cottage cheese with blueberries on it that's up to the finest table set by the rich. Are refuges and compensations travel, sailboats, jewelry? What do the rich have that you and I have to discover for ourselves? Certainly not strength of character, sticking power, or some other inner resource.

Fitzgerald was just coming down from *The Great Gatsby* (1925) and waiting for it to be published when he wrote "The Rich Boy." He had a lot of feelings about the rich left over, that he'd not gotten into *Gatsby*. He knew that in Jay Gatsby himself he'd not really said very much about the rich, nor in Tom and Daisy Buchanan. What's more, in cutting the Rudolph Miller prologue, and another long passage about Gatsby's early affair with Daisy, he also sensed something hollow about his hero, something missing in the finished book now on its way to the printers. Rudolph Miller would not have told us much about Gatsby, but Fitzgerald, nonetheless, felt he'd not done the picture of great wealth he'd meant to do. Now he would do it.

The opening tells us that Fitzgerald is about to do an original character study that shows us the rich as we have never seen them. Fitzgerald sets out to give us the pathology of a rich boy, as he did that of a priest, in "Absolution." But this full-blown, three-paragraph opening, unlike that sensuous opening which drops us right into the priest's illness, could open a novel or novelette but would disfigure a short story. Fitzgerald saw "The Rich Boy" as a novelette and published it (after his regular outlet the high-paying *Saturday Evening Post* turned thumbs down) in two parts in *Redbook* magazine, a cut in income he had to accept for writing honestly.

Could we cut the first paragraph? Start with "There are no types, no plurals. There is a rich boy . . . ?" Perhaps. But then we'd leave out ". . . we are all queer fish, queerer behind our faces and voices than we want any one to know or than we know ourselves," which exactly captures this selfish rich boy's superior-mindedness, and heartlessness, toward others—and is pricelessly well put. Yet, still unsatisfied, Fitzgerald once again—in Dick and Nicole Diver of *Tender Is the Night* (1934)—will gird himself for a deeper picture of the rich, show us how wealth seemingly assures character, bestows culture, and releases Dick's genius . . . before money eats Dick alive, and before his drinking, his lost hopes as a psychologist, and the couple's adulteries sink their marriage. However, this picture of the rich sketches Fitzgerald's own life, not that of Gerald and Sara Murphy—some highly cultured Riviera party-givers on whom he'd meant to base his story—before his own tragedies took over the plot. The Murphys, whose charmed lives faded with the deaths of their two teenaged sons, disliked his having used them as "scrap granite" for his novel. "I can't help wishing we were in some other book," Sara said.

We would also lose Fitzgerald's whispered hint that he will show us a rounded person, not a flat type, an unspoken pledge (if only to himself) that he'll go all out this time. And he does, within the limits of a magazine novelette. The opening makes clear the storyteller's rights to the reader's confidence, "All my life I have lived among his brothers but this one has been my friend." He knows that the rich we most often read about seem unreal to us, so he's going to tell us not just about the rich, but the very rich. Then come his grand charges against them: They are soft where we are hard, cynical where we are trustful, in ways hard to grasp. Deep in their hearts they think they're better than us—and even if they lose their money, they think that! They are different.

Fitzgerald will show us just what a foreigner to the middle class a rich boy is and how his words and sentences are "all very crisp and clear and not run together as ours are" and have an acquired accent "that is peculiar to fashionable people in the city of New York." You're now into the fourth paragraph, so you'd better find the book and keep going.

> I am an invisible man. No, I am not a spook like those who haunted Edgar Allan Poe; nor am I one of your Hollywood-movie ectoplasms. I am a man of substance, of flesh and bone, fiber and liquids—and I might even be said to possess a mind. I am invisible, understand, simply because people refuse to see me. Like the bodiless heads you see sometimes in circus sideshows, it is as though I have been surrounded by mirrors of hard, distorting glass. When they approach me they see only my surroundings, themselves, or figments of their imagination—indeed, everything and anything except me.
>
> —*Invisible Man* (1952), Ralph Ellison

You may never have seen a circus sideshow where a man or woman sits above you on a chair and seemingly has no head—a trick done with mirrors. The nameless black storyteller of *Invisible Man* likening himself to a head with no body makes the theme of this novel so searing that most readers can't take it in at first; I certainly didn't back in 1952. Nearly forty years later, the bodiless black man of the first paragraph still eats and sleeps in a living death that I *once* took as a mere literary trick to make thinking about it bearable. Perhaps the novel's brilliant humor and surrealism blinded me (or that was all I was looking for). The underground world of the Invisible Man was so raw and new to me that I could accept it only as showy device, to be measured against *Of Time and the River* and *The Great Gatsby*, then my benchmarks of American prose. The novel's bare-nerved livingness went by me.

Today, I feel that it offers one of the firmest handshakes that I will ever know and speaks with a voice that softens any edginess I may feel. It grips me and says, Come in, welcome to my castle cellar. I learn, at once, that the Invisible Man lives in an underground "hole," or rather a walled-off coal cellar that divorces him from Manhattan. His only tie with others is by way of bootlegging electrical power from Monopolated Light & Power, "juice" he uses to become visible to himself by turning on the 1,369 light bulbs in his ceiling—and he's already adding sockets to a wall. He puts on Louis Armstrong's recording of

> *What did I do*
> *To be so black*
> *And blue?*

and then tells me how being invisible allows him to see around corners and do other feats, but he's been down here hibernating too long, getting his mind together and setting himself up to do something that speaks for his manhood. Liketa tell you my story, how for twenty years I never knew I was alive until I discovered I was invisible. . . . His story is about blackness making him two people, a well-schooled youth born to American idealism who can go on breathing only by cutting loose from the social illusions which keep him in a caste system—and this invisible man who relishes the richness of life on the bottom, the spunk of the underdogs, and the new freedom to love himself that a life of invisibility grants him.

I think everyone's favorite section is the nighttime Harlem race riot where the bewildered hero, being chased, finds himself trying to hail a cab. "Then three men in natty cream-colored summer suits came to stand near me at the curb, and something about them struck me like a hammer. They were all wearing dark glasses. I had seen it thousands of times, but suddenly what I had considered an empty imitation of a Hollywood fad was flooded with personal significance." He rushes into a drug store, buys dark glasses "of a green glass so dark that it appeared black, and I put them on immediately, plunging into blackness and moving outside. I could barely see . . . the street swarmed in a green vagueness." Then he hurries into a hat shop, buys the most wide-brimmed zoot suit hat in the store, goes back out and is taken for the coolest dude in the riot. "What you sayin', daddy-o?"

Invisible Man is challenged only by Alice Walker's *The Color Purple* as the great American black novel. Ellison's second novel, again and again said to be nearly done, is now the most long-awaited work of fiction—forty years! Chapters of it, seen here and there in small magazines, give every promise of an inspired work, one that will shake our spines.

> In the fall the war was always there, but we did not go to it any more. It was cold in the fall in Milan and the dark came very early. Then the electric lights came on, and it was pleasant along the streets looking in the windows. There was much game hanging outside the shops, and the snow powdered in the fur of the foxes and the wind blew their tails. The deer hung stiff and heavy and empty, and small birds blew in the wind and the wind turned their feathers. It was a cold fall and the wind came down from the mountains.
> —"In Another Country" (1927), *The Complete Short Stories of Ernest Hemingway* (1987)

Why is this sheer magic? Perhaps, at first, it isn't. I read that paragraph for many years before it bloomed for me. I was always taken by its plain words, one might say pure Anglo-Saxon, which will not lose a breath of their freshness for hundreds of years. Even so, it took years before their sensuous chill went up my nose and down my nerves.

What is this paragraph doing? First, setting the war mood, the feelings of the hero as his war wound heals and he undergoes physical rebuilding. These are not only a feeling of apartness brought on by his wound and hospitalization, but also of being in a country other than his homeland. Then it's the natural melancholy of the time of year, and of wartime itself, and the war in which he no longer fights, and also of the sadness of these dead animals he sees, unspokenly bringing to mind the dead at the front—dead he has seen, dead who were comrades, the fresh dead still stretched out where they fall. The birds strike us strongly as they blow in the wind and the wind turns their feathers. The Italians eat sparrows—or did. Are these small birds dead game or live and blowing about in the sky or perhaps hopping about in the street? I think they're strung up. The title echoes the irony of Christopher Marlowe's famous lines from *The Jew of Malta*: "But that was in another country/And besides the wench is dead"—just as sex is dead for these maimed soldiers living with the hero. The title adds a bloom of poetry to this paragraph which points up the three-beat rhythms that run through the second sentence: "It was *cold* in the *fall* in *Milan*:" the muted two-beat rhythms of blank verse: the hard double accents (snow powdered, birds blew) followed by three-beat phrases, with the deathsong "It was a *cold fall* and the *wind* came *down* from the *mountains*."

Careful about rhythms, Hemingway had earlier published some verse of no great worth and also his heroic, icy-clear, italicized one-paragraph chapter headings for *in our time* (1924):

They shot the six cabinet ministers at half-past six in the morning against the wall of a hospital. There were pools of water in the courtyard. There were wet dead leaves on the paving of the courtyard. It rained hard. All the shutters of the hospital were nailed shut. One of the ministers was sick with typhoid. Two soldiers carried him downstairs and out into the rain. They tried to hold him up against the wall but he sat down in a puddle of water. The other five stood very quietly against the wall. Finally the officer told the soldiers it was no good trying to make him stand up. When they fired the first volley he was sitting down in the water with his head on his knees.

　　　　—Chapter V, *in our time* (1924), Ernest Hemingway

That scans nicely, with Hemingway using many, but not too many, three-beat rhythms for an echo of verse, and hard sentence stops to dampen them. He was a journalist and knew that in reporting an incident, like the shooting of six cabinet ministers, you do not write "There were pools of water in the courtyard. There were wet dead leaves on the paving of the courtyard." You write, "Pools of water stood in the courtyard. Wet leaves lay on the paving." You don't use extra syllables such as "There were," or repeat "of the courtyard" and "in the courtyard." And all fallen leaves are dead. If you say "wet dead leaves" for "wet leaves," it's poetry. And the third, stinging "against the wall" would be cut by a news editor. Even so, this war sketch, and other small acid sketches like it, in *in our time* were seen as stunningly compressed—and likened to Goya's "The Disasters of War." His bitter originality was weighed and found to be "absolute genius," with his words striking one reviewer "as if the language were being made over." It's good to remember just what a bombshell Hemingway's voice was in 1924 and 1925. Within years, all America was trying to imitate it and failing. Even his friend, Fitzgerald, fought against its hard pull. What was imitated was his mannered understatement, especially in dialogue, and the look of a Hemingway paragraph, a cynical voice and small, sharp words in flat statements. What his imitators didn't see was that he was not a reporter. He had, in fact, not seen the shooting of the six cabinet ministers but, rather, had taken it from the London *Times*, changed the time of the execution from noon to dawn, put in the wet dead leaves, ironically added the hospital shutters being nailed shut, and made a work of art out of an event supposedly seen first hand.

Now watch these leaves as he uses them four years later:

> In the late summer of that year we lived in a house in a village that looked across the river and the plain to the mountains. In the bed of the river there were pebbles and boulders, dry and white in the sun, and the water was clear and swiftly moving and blue in the channels. Troops went by the house and down the road and the dust they raised **powdered the leaves of the trees. The trunks of the trees too were dusty and the leaves fell early that year and we saw the troops** marching along the road and the dust rising and leaves, stirred by the breeze, falling and the soldiers marching and afterward the road bare and white except for the leaves.
>
> —*A Farewell to Arms* (1929), Ernest Hemingway

Now the wet dead leaves that foretold the deaths of the six cabinet ministers are powdered with dust. The leaves (soldiers) fell early that year, and we saw the troops marching along the road, the dust rising, and leaves, stirred by the breeze, falling; the soldiers marching and, afterward, the road bare and white, except for the leaves.

How do you like that?

Here the cadences from the shooting of the six cabinet ministers are loosened and lifted, they hover, the beat barely stirring the dust, and all's hanging while the leaves fall and soldiers march and the dust rises and the leaves, stirred by the breezes of war, fall and the soldiers march and then the road is bare and white, except for the fallen.

What can't be imitated here is the singingly high pitch at which Hemingway has set this casual rise and fall of dust and leaves and death. This is not the same pitch or mood as "In Another Country," where "it was cold in the fall in Milan and the dark came very early. Then the electric lights came on, and it was pleasant along the streets looking in the windows. There was much game hanging outside the shops, and the snow powdered in the fur of the foxes and the wind blew their tails. The deer hung stiff and heavy and empty, and small birds blew in the wind and the wind turned their feathers. It was a cold fall and the wind came down from the mountains."

Not the same. By the fourth sentence of *Farewell*, Hemingway tells that a leaf is a leaf is a leaf so well that he can abandon simple statement and lift off into heavenly repetition with a sentence that has seven subjects. Why does it work? Well, the paragraph opens wide-angle in soft song, as if committing itself to things lasting in nature: Ever-Returning summer, a house, a village, the river, the plain, the mountains. Then it clears the eye, as if focusing a just-polished lens, and takes us into textures and colors, the sunstruck bed of the river with pebbles and boulders, dry and white in the sun, and the water clear and swiftly moving and blue in the channels. This is what we have in nature that we can lose. The quality of life in Hemingway's up-close surfaces of the pebbles and boulders, and the one drop of color he splashes onto his paragraph, the swiftly moving blue water, is what the soldiers leave behind as they march through the dust powdering the trunks of the trees, becoming fallen leaves on the road bare of man and white except for the leaves. A tragic sadness felt against the piercing immediacy of nature gives this paragraph its power, along with the perfect sentence rhythms and fearless grammar that underpins their march into bare, white death. These qualities, for me, place it at the very peak of the first paragraphs we've looked over.

Where could that voice go from there? Twenty-three years later:

> He was an old man who fished alone in a skiff in the
> Gulf Stream and he had gone eighty-four days now without
> taking a fish. In the first forty days a boy had been with

him. But after forty days without a fish the boy's parents had told him that the old man was now definitely and finally *salao*, which is the worst form of unlucky, and the boy had gone at their orders in another boat which caught three good fish the first week. It made the boy sad to see the old man come in each day with his skiff empty and he always went down to help him carry either the coiled lines or the gaff and harpoon and the sail that was furled around the mast. The sail was patched with flour sacks and, furled, it looked like the flag of permanent defeat.

　　—*The Old Man and the Sea* (1952), Ernest Hemingway

The thirty-one-year-old writer's tension and vibrance are taken over by heightened eloquence and the sounds of a fifty-four-year-old storyteller filling us in with broad strokes of background. In his youth, Hemingway suggests more than he tells, places us right next to the war which looms and booms just beyond the mountains. Now, the great tensions are in the past, and the old man faces the last big battle that will make impossible demands on his wisdom and skill. The rhythms make up longer, less daring sentences, loosened to a more easeful tension.

Here is the sound which fills the paragraph: fished, skiff, Gulf, eighty-four, fish, first forty, after forty, fish, definitely and finally, form, fish, first, skiff, gaff, furled, flour, furled, flag, defeat. Formality replaces "they shot the six cabinet ministers at half-past six in the morning and the wind came down from the mountains and the leaves fell early that year." Now, we get the aging bass-baritone who will rely on vocalizing rather than power, and he is "an old man who fishes alone in a skiff on the Gulf Stream and he has gone eighty-four days now without taking a fish." Where are my gold records? the great recording star asks. My platinum celebrity that I could always rely on in the tough places? After a terrible pasting from the reviewers, who wiped the canvas with the champ for

Across the River and into the Trees (1950), he went on with *The Old Man and the Sea* but his voice, hard-edged and warlike only yesterday, had aged overnight. He wrote in a letter: "It will be nice to win after the shit I had to eat about the last book." He won, but *The Old Man and the Sea* is wonderful only in part and in long passages and has many forced notes, sentimental weaknesses, and a leadenly ironic last scene with a falseness that wounds like a sharkbite. But we will suffer these for the great picture we are given of the sea and the various fish who live in it. Hemingway's flag may be patched but it remains undefeated.

How shall we end our book? Why not with the greatest first paragraph ever written?

> When all things began, the Word already was. The Word dwelt with God, and what God was, the Word was. The Word, then, was with God at the beginning, and through him all things came to be; no single thing was created without him. All that came to be was alive with his life, and that life was the light of men. The light shines on in the dark, and the darkness has never quenched it.
> —"The Gospel According to John," *The New English Bible* (1965)

Eternity—what a canvas!

Who wrote this? Nobody knows. Scholarship points this way and that and changes its mind every fifty years, but being Nameless isn't so bad when you write like this.

After this brief prologue, the story gets down to earth and tells of the coming of Christ. But Nameless wants a big opening before he gives us the facts. Scholarship tells us that he lived in Ephesus, an Asian city now called Izmir in Turkey, and wrote in Greek in the late first century. This means he's certainly read Homer and Homer's smiting of the anvil as he calls on the Muse to help him open *The Iliad*:

Sing for me, Muse, the mania of Achilles
that cast a thousand sorrows on the Greeks
and threw so many huge souls into hell,
heroes who spilled their lives as food for dogs
and darting birds. God's will was working out,
from that time when first fell apart fighting
Atrides, king of men, and that god, Achilles . . .
—*Imitations* (1961), Robert Lowell

Nameless needs the right sound, the right words, something even bigger than Homer. In fact, bigger than Moses and Genesis and *In the beginning God created the heavens and the earth. The earth was without form and void, and darkness was upon the face of the deep; and the Spirit of God was moving over the face of the waters.* He's got to pitch this one very high. And so, he calls on Jesus, and Jesus enlightens him. Who am I? Jesus asks—or answers—Nameless. I am the Word. Before all things began, I already was, and dwelt with God. I, the Word, was with God at the beginning, and through my Word all things came to be. No single thing was created without me. All that came to be was alive with my life, and my life was the light of men. My light shines on in the dark, and the darkness has never quenched it.

Nameless has only to catch these words on the wing but once, and down they go. He sits entranced by a Word at the heart of the universe. A *great* opening—it will shed light over every word that follows. And he thanks Jesus, whose light shines on in the dark.

And may yours.

Sit back. Open your mind. Let power, wisdom, and love be your first principle. Hold up your hammer. Say, first paragraph, first principle. As you strike your first paragraph, remember Dickens: "Implacable November weather. As much mud in the streets as if the waters had but newly retired from the face of the earth." Remember Melville: "Call me Ishmael." Remember Proust: "Time and again, I have gone to bed early.

Often enough, my candle just out, my eyes would close even before I had time to realize, 'I'm falling asleep'." Remember Fitzgerald: "There was once a priest with cold, watery eyes, who, in the still of the night, wept cold tears." Remember Doctorow: "In 1902 Father built a house at the crest of the Broadview Avenue hill in New Rochelle, New York." Remember Stead: "All the June Saturday afternoon Sam Pollit's children were on the lookout for him as they skated round the dirt sidewalks and seamed old asphalt of R Street and Reservoir Road that bounded the deep-grassed acres of Tohoga House, their home." Remember Poe: "The thousand injuries of Fortunato I had borne as best I could; but when he ventured upon insult, I vowed revenge." Remember Ellison: "I am an invisible man." Remember Joyce: "riverrun, past Eve and Adam's, from swerve of shore to bend of bay, brings us by a commodius vicus of recirculation back to Howth Castle and Environs." Remember Plath: "It was a queer, sultry summer, the summer they electrocuted the Rosenbergs, and I didn't know what I was doing in New York. I'm stupid about executions." Remember Burroughs: "I can feel the heat closing in, feel them out there making their moves." Remember Salinger: "If you really want to hear about it, the first thing you'll probably want to know is where I was born, and what my lousy childhood was like, and how my parents were occupied and all before they had me, and all that David Copperfield kind of crap, but I don't feel like going into it, if you want to know the truth." Remember O'Connor: "Francis Marion Tarwater's uncle had been dead for only half a day when the boy got too drunk to finish digging his grave and a Negro named Buford Munson, who had come to get a jug filled, had to finish it and drag the body from the breakfast table where it was still sitting and bury it in a decent and Christian way, with the sign of its Saviour at the head of the grave and enough dirt on top to keep the dogs from digging it up." Remember Kennedy: "Riding up the winding road of Saint Agnes Cemetery in the back of the rattling old truck, Francis Phelan became aware that the dead,

even more than the living, settled down in neighborhoods."
Remember Faulkner: "Through the bloody September twilight, aftermath of sixty-two rainless days, it had gone like a fire in dry grass—the rumor, the story, whatever it was."
Remember Mailer: "On a late winter evening in 1983, while driving through fog along the Maine coast, recollections of old campfires began to drift through the March mist, and I thought of the Abnaki Indians of the Algonquin tribe who dwelt near Bangor a thousand years ago." Remember Brodkey: "I was slapped and hurried along in the private applause of birth—I think I remember this." Remember Cain: "They threw me off the hay truck about noon." Remember Updike: "Men emerge pale from the little printing plant at four sharp, ghosts for an instant, blinking, until the outdoor light overcomes the look of constant indoor light clinging to them." Remember Welty: "It was late afternoon, with heavy silver clouds which looked bigger and wider than cotton fields, and presently it began to rain." Remember Wylie: "It was nearly sunset. High above the broad valley gigantic shafts of mellowing sunlight slanted down majestically to earth." Remember Young: "The bus-driver was whistling, perhaps in anticipation of his wife, who would be a woman with ample breasts, those of a realized maturity." Remember Dinesen: "I had a farm in Africa, at the foot of the Ngong Hills." Remember T. E. Lawrence: "Some of the evil of my tale may have been inherent in our circumstances. For years we lived anyhow with one another in the naked desert, under the indifferent heaven." Remember McCullers: "It happened that green and crazy summer when Frankie was twelve years old." Remember Miller: "Once you have given up the ghost, everything follows with dead certainty, even in the midst of chaos." Remember McInerney: "IT'S SIX A.M. DO YOU KNOW WHERE YOU ARE? You are not the kind of guy who would be at a place like this at this time of the morning." Remember Giono: "It was an extraordinary night. The wind had been blowing; it had ceased, and the stars had sprouted like weeds." Remember

Crane: "None of them knew the color of the sky." Remember Pynchon: "A screaming comes across the sky." Remember Nabokov: "Lolita, light of my life, fire of my loins. My sin, my soul." Remember Markham: "How is it possible to bring order out of memory?" Remember Bellow: "What made me take this trip to Africa? There is no quick explanation." Remember Kafka: "During these last decades the interest in professional fasting has markedly diminished." Remember Tolstoy: "The Assyrian King, Esarhaddon, had conquered the kingdom of King Lailie, had destroyed and burnt the towns, taken all the inhabitants captive to his own country, slaughtered the warriors, beheaded some chieftains and impaled or flayed others, and had confined King Lailie himself in a cage." Remember Garcia Marquez: "Many years later, as he faced the firing squad, Colonel Aureliano Buendia was to remember that distant afternoon when his father took him to discover ice."

And remember:

"They shot the six cabinet ministers at half-past six in the morning against the wall of a hospital."

Not at six-thirty in the morning, but at HALF-PAST SIX, three hard beats. Wet dead leaves, three hard beats. It rained hard, three hard beats, all the shutters of the hospital were nailed shut. NAILED SHUT.

Remember: Writing can get you fed to a lion whose teeth draw your whole face into its foul wet breath and cut your skull with knives. There's no soft way to put this. A black hole swallows you up. Willpower's no help. Getting in print is like beating cancer but losing a lung, staying in print is hopeless. Your best work goes begging. Short stuff has no market. Whatever checks show up—late—you brace at once against the toppling rent and insurance. One by one, your kids in print are pulped, your manuscript trunk feels full of backbreaking anchor chain, or bodies awaiting Christ, your work's shot down monthly by editors, agents give up on you, and you feed off whatever you write today. *That's* the big loaf that never dies. Today's paragraph comes, a word from the heart of the universe, and shines in the darkness, unquenched.

And you ask for power, wisdom, and love as you make the anvil sing.

Valentine's Day, 1991
GREENWICH VILLAGE